T I M E B E N I E

+ T S N U K

N E N N I : R E L T S N Ü K

T R I X + R O B E R T

N N A M S U A H

I M G E S P R Ä C H

T I M

D I E T E R S C H W A R Z

W I L H

I N C O N V E R S A T I O N

H A U S M A N N

T R I X + R O B E R T

A R T I S T S

A R T +

A L L T I W I L H

E D I T I O N

P A T R I C K

F R E Y

N ° 3 3 8

# EIN LEBEN MIT DER KUNST
## UND KÜNSTLER:INNEN
### TRIX [TH] UND ROBERT HAUSSMANN [RH]
### IM GESPRÄCH MIT DIETER SCHWARZ [DS]

DS    Betritt man die Wohnung von Robert und
Trix Haussmann, dann befindet man sich zwischen
Spiegeln, die einem zunächst die Orientierung er-
schweren, und man denkt an die Aussage der beiden,
dass man mit Spiegeln die Realität zerstören, aus-
dehnen und verändern könne. Dasselbe gilt in ande-
rem Sinne, meine ich, auch für die Zeichnungen und
Bilder, welche die Wände dicht bedecken, und die
Plastiken, die überall stehen, wo zwischen Büchern
und Gegenständen ein Platz frei ist. Gibt es ein Prin-
zip für die Hängung, wie oft wird sie geändert?

TH    Wir haben stets versucht, die Bilder so zu
hängen, dass sie innerlich zusammenpassen, dass aber
auch ihre Formate miteinander korrelieren – ein Werk
sollte mit dem anderen sprechen. Die Hängung war
jeweils eine grosse Anstrengung, doch wenn wir in der
Wohnung etwas renovierten oder wenn mehrere Wer-
ke ausgeliehen waren, mussten wir halt umhängen.

DS    Verstehen Sie sich als Kunstsammler?

TH    Eigentlich nicht.

RH    Wenn man alt wird und wenn die Dinge,
die einen interessieren und betreffen, um einen ver-
sammelt sind, dann ergibt sich so etwas wie eine
Sammlung.

TH    In erster Linie ging es um Freundschaften; man kannte Künstler:innen, und daraus entstand manches. Dann war es auch ein Ausgleich zur eigenen Arbeit als Architekt:innen. Wir hatten stets einen Auftraggeber, und die Künstler:innen waren der Gegenpol – sie konnten etwas frei und ohne Verpflichtung herstellen. Das war für uns, die im Auftrag kreativ arbeiteten, ein anregender Aspekt.

DS    Kamen Sie im Zusammenhang mit Ihrer Ausbildung zur bildenden Kunst, oder war Ihr Interesse schon früher geweckt worden?

RH    Für mich begann es zum Zeitpunkt des Übergangs von der Kindheit ins Erwachsenenalter. In der Klee-Ausstellung im Kunsthaus Zürich von 1948 war ich zum ersten Mal von Kunst überwältigt. Am Sonntagnachmittag gab es im Kunsthaus freien Eintritt, und da ich in der Nähe wohnte, trieb ich mich ganze Nachmittage in der Museumssammlung herum. Es war so, wie andere ins Kino gehen, etwas Unbelastetes, das sich vom Elternhaus unterschied.

DS    Hatten Sie zu Hause schon Kontakt mit Kunstwerken?

RH    Zu Hause nicht, aber als ich studierte, machte ich vor dem Diplom ein Austauschjahr in Amsterdam und verbrachte auch ein paar Monate in Schwe-

den. Gerrit Rietveld war damals der Direktor der Kunstnijverheidsschool (Kunstgewerbeschule) in Amsterdam; dank ihm wurde ich mit Willem Sandberg bekannt, der Direktor des Stedelijk Museum war und 1951 die erste De-Stijl-Ausstellung veranstaltete. Ich durfte mich als Praktikant mit Briefen, Skizzen und anderen Dokumenten befassen, die bei verschiedensten Nachlässen eingesammelt und korbweise in das Museum gebracht wurden.

DS    Sandberg hatte nach dem Krieg das Stedelijk Museum zum führenden Museum in Europa gemacht ...

RH    ... und in Amsterdam war auch das Concertgebouw Orchestra, es gab nicht nur die Grachten. Für die De-Stijl-Ausstellung wurde aus einem Nachlass eine schwer beschädigte Zeichnung von Theo van Doesburg angeliefert; sie war auf Transparentpapier ausgeführt und hatte starke braune Flecken. Ich kaufte Talens-Farben, mischte sie an und versuchte jeden einzelnen Flecken zu retuschieren. Als wir Jahre später in New York eine Ausstellung im Museum of Modern Art besuchten, sahen wir ein Blatt, das fürchterlich aussah, es war das von mir «restaurierte»; das Papier und die Retuschen hatten sich verfärbt, und es sah schlimmer aus als zuvor.

DS    Mit Klee und den Künstlern von De Stijl hatten sie bereits zentrale Figuren der Moderne kennengelernt. Hatten Sie in Zürich Lehrer, die Sie auf solche Künstler:innen hinwiesen?

RH    Direktor der Kunstgewerbeschule war Johannes Itten, der aus dem Bauhaus kam, aber in seinen Vorlesungen esoterische Theorien propagierte. Das war wie schon am Bauhaus – Atemübungen ergänzten seine Farbenlehre.

DS    Sie hatten Ihre Ausbildung an der Kunstgewerbeschule und nicht an der Architekturabteilung der ETH in Zürich gemacht?

RH    Ich kam aber mit einigen Professoren der ETH in Kontakt. Besonders ragte Sigfried Giedion hervor, der um sich einen Kreis von Student:innen geschart hatte und in seiner Villa im Doldertal einen Salon führte. Man war da zum Tee, und jeder musste einmal einen kurzen Vortrag halten. Man setzte sich mit aktuellen Fragen wie der Proportionslehre oder neuer Musik auseinander und kam mit manchen Dingen in Berührung. So legte Wladimir Vogel, dessen Sprechchöre damals Aufsehen erregten, die Zwölftontechnik dar, und Hans Kayser dozierte seine esoterische Lehre von der allumfassenden, vom Planetensystem abgeleiteten Harmonik. Wir bauten nach seinen Anweisungen ein Monochord, eine Art

Musikinstrument mit zwölf gleichgestimmten Saiten, um damit die Proportionen zu veranschaulichen.

TH    Kaysers Gedanken waren damals auch für Architekt:innen wichtig; ich erhielt zum Studienbeginn von meiner Tante ein Buch von Kayser.

RH    Besonders bewunderte ich die Sammlung der Giedions, die sich nahtlos in die Fülle von Büchern einfügte. Ich war sehr begeisterungsfähig, und umgekehrt begeisterte dies die Älteren. Hans Arp und andere Künstler:innen waren ab und zu zu Gast. Als Studenten einmal ihre Vorträge hielten, fragte Giedion ihn: «Arp, was meinen Sie dazu?» Da nahm Arp, der ein Raucher war, eine Streichholzschachtel aus der Tasche, warf die Streichhölzer auf den Tisch und sagte: «Das ist doch schön!» Dann sammelte er sie ein, warf sie erneut hin und sagte: «Jetzt ist es wieder schön.» Davon war ich tief beeindruckt, und die Einsicht in die Gesetze des Zufalls wirkte viel später in meiner eigenen Arbeit weiter.

DS    Wie war Carola Giedion-Welcker präsent?

RH    Mit der neuen Literatur, die sie vermittelte, und dadurch, dass sie so viele bedeutende Künstler:innen kannte. Nach meiner Ausbildung war ich für kurze Zeit Assistent von Willy Rotzler, der damals das Kunstgewerbemuseum leitete. Ich half ihm,

Ausstellungen aufzubauen, beispielsweise 1952 die Ausstellung *Angewandte Kunst aus Dänemark*, an der ich die dänischen Designer kennenlernte.

DS    Und wie kamen Sie zur Kunst?

TH    Ich bin in Bern in einer vom Bauhaus geprägten Umgebung aufgewachsen; wir hatten Breuer-Stühle, und meine Eltern waren mit Künstler:innen befreundet. Mein Vater ging mit uns in Bern um die Weihnachtszeit an die sogenannte Kramgasse-Ausstellung, bei der jeder Laden in seinem Schaufenster Bilder zeigte. Im Gymnasium war ich eine begabte Zeichenschülerin. Mit etwa fünfzehn lernte ich durch meine Eltern Walter und Margrit Linck kennen, und ich durfte in ihrem Atelier Keramik bemalen. Eigentlich durften im Atelier nur Männer töpfern, und die Frauen bemalten die Keramik. Walter Lincks Werk und Persönlichkeit beeindruckten mich tief, und ich nahm zuerst gar nicht wahr, dass Margrit Linck auch als Künstlerin tätig war.

Mich beeindruckte, dass es bei den Lincks keinen hässlichen Gegenstand gab – die Räume waren einfach schön. An der Aussenwand des Ateliers wuchs eine Rebe, und – ob sie nun Trauben trug oder nicht – Linck fand, dass sie Trauben haben sollte, und kaufte künstliche Trauben, die er daran befestigte. Ich begriff, dass man etwas Schönes herstellen konnte, auch wenn man sich nicht an die Regeln hielt.

Als ich später beim Architekten Rudolf Olgiati arbeitete, fand ich diese Idee der Schönheit wieder. Ihm galt die optische Wirklichkeit mehr als die Materialgerechtigkeit, mit der ich aufgewachsen war; er war ein Antipode des Unterrichts, den wir an der ETH erhalten hatten. Olgiati richtete im Gästezimmer eine Bibliothek ein, die er weiss strich, und da ihn der violette Leineneinband von Carl Spittelers *Olympischem Frühling* störte, strich er auch diesen weiss an.

RH    Das Trompe-l'œil hat dich also schon damals beschäftigt. Zum Ausdruck kam es dann wirklich in unserer Stoffkollektion von 1981 für die Textilfirma Mira-X, als wir architektonische Grundmuster als *faux-marbre* oder *faux-bois* auf Stoffe übertrugen – unserer vielleicht wichtigsten Arbeit überhaupt.

TH    Zuerst aber begann ich an der ETH in Zürich das Studium der Architektur. Dann heiratete ich, hatte zwei Kinder, und ich zog mit meinem ersten Mann in die USA und nach Mexiko. Während dieser Zeit spielte die Kunst keine wichtige Rolle, ausser in Mexiko, wo ich dem Werk des Architekten Luis Barragán in der Casa Pedregal mit ihren starken Farben begegnete. Nach meiner Rückkehr begann ich erneut mit dem Architekturstudium und brachte es zu Ende. Eine wichtige Anregung war die Vorlesung über den Manierismus von Adolf Max Vogt;

sie eröffnete mir einen ganz anderen Zugang zur Kunst.

DS      Und wie sind Sie sich dann begegnet?

TH      An der Expo 64 in Lausanne, wo ich als frisch diplomierte Architektin im Büro Gisel Howald Schnebli am Bau des Centre de l'Hôtellerie arbeitete, für das Robert das Restaurant gestaltete und einen Stuhl entwarf.

RH      Nach der Begegnung an der Lausanner Expo 64 sahen wir uns 1966 an einer Luginbühl-Ausstellung in der Galerie Ziegler in Zürich wieder. 1967 heirateten wir und gründeten ein gemeinsames Entwurfsbüro. Wir stellten fest, dass wir ähnliche Interessen hatten, beispielsweise für den italienischen Manierismus.

DS      Das waren aber konträre Gebiete – auf der einen Seite das Konstruktive auf dem Hintergrund von De Stijl oder Walter Linck und auf der anderen Seite der Manierismus. Wie haben Sie das zusammengebracht?

TH      Wir haben zwar mit Trompe-l'œil-Effekten, Spiegeln, virtuellen Räumen gearbeitet, aber dafür bauten wir stets ein festes Fundament.

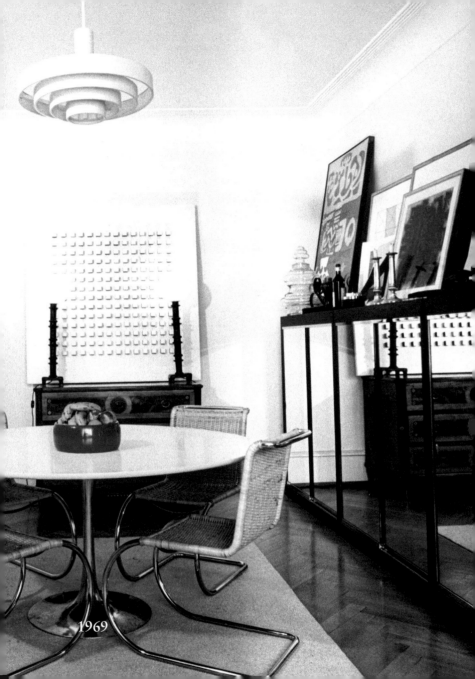

1969

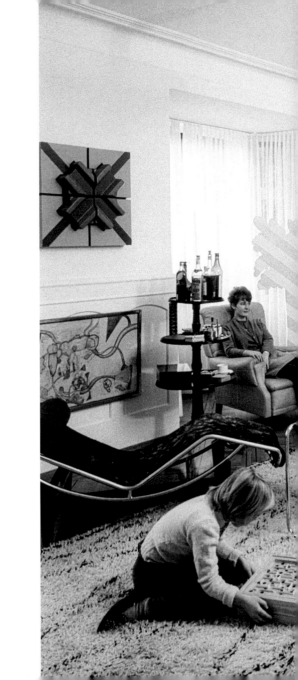

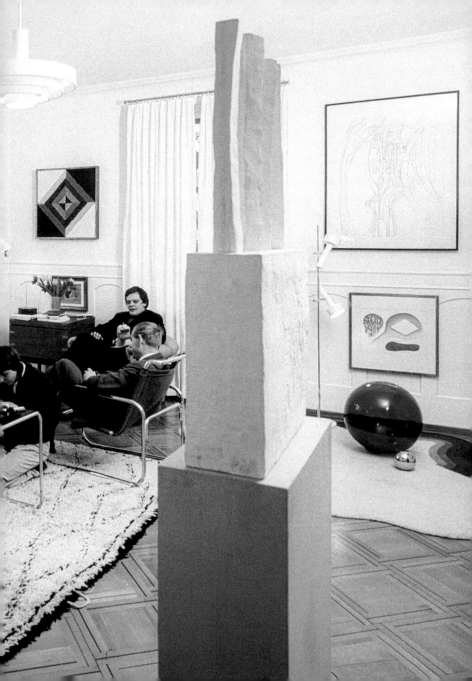

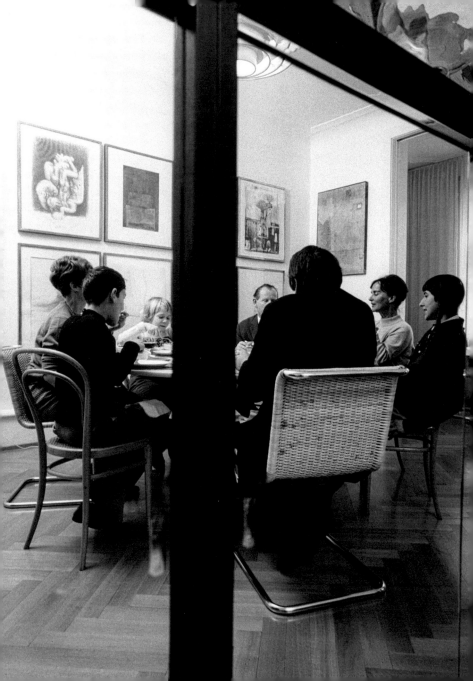

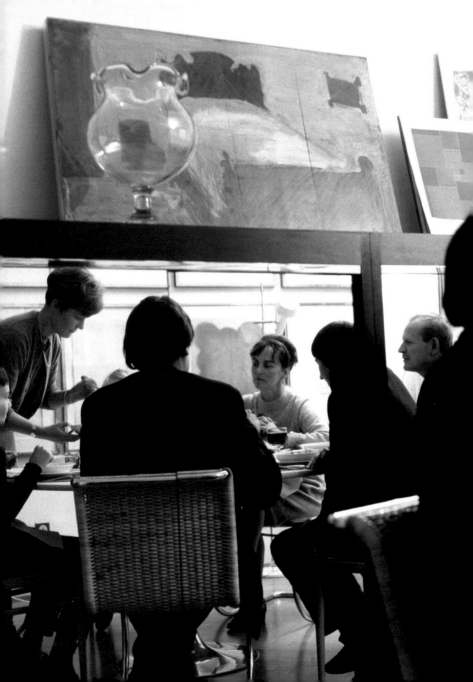

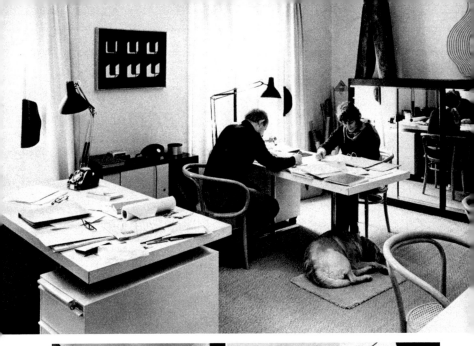

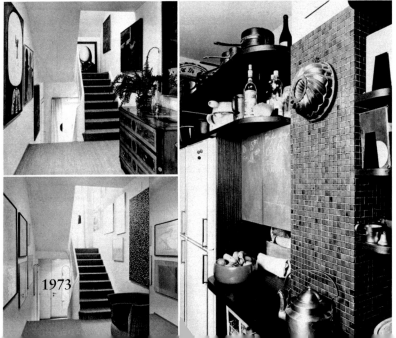

1973

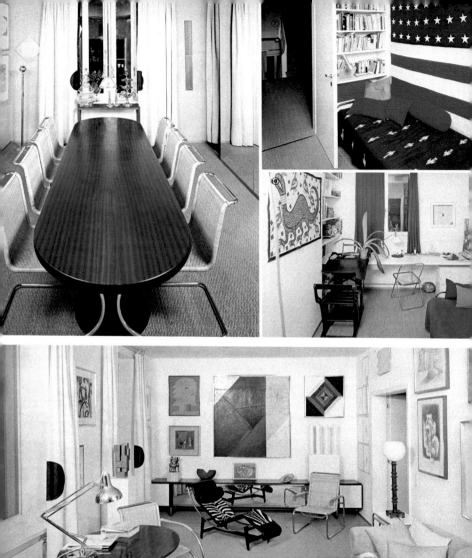
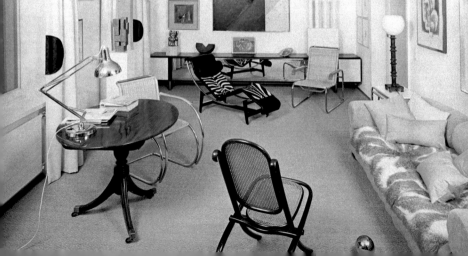

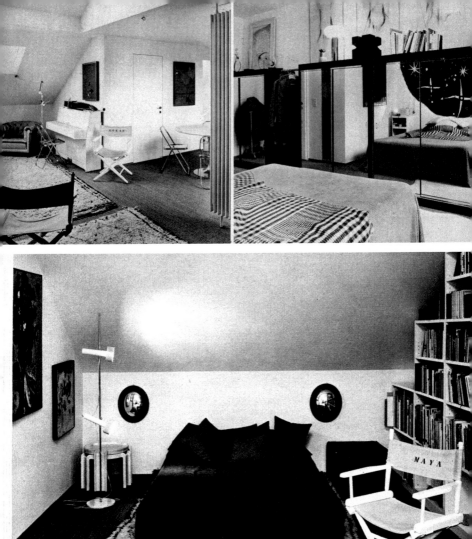
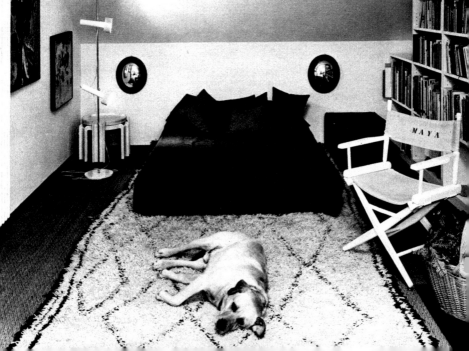

<sup>DS</sup> Und wie sind Sie aus dem Giedion-Kreis
zum Manierismus gelangt?

<sup>RH</sup>     Zu Hause fand ich auf dem Estrich tschechi-
sche Avantgardezeitschriften aus den 1920er-Jahren,
und darin entdeckte ich ein Bild von Friedrich Vordemberge-Gildewart, in dem die konstruktive Kom-
position durch das Anbringen von Holz-, Metall-
und Glaselementen aufgebrochen war. Als ich in
Amsterdam studierte, besuchte ich ihn und zeigte
ihm diese Abbildung. Ich empfand die plastischen
Elemente auf den Bildern nicht als manieristisch,
sondern als Erweiterung der Bauhaus-Moderne.

<sup>DS</sup>     Spielten im Giedion-Kreis auch Max Bill
und Richard Paul Lohse eine Rolle?

<sup>RH</sup>     Nein. Mit Bill war ich nie wirklich befreun-
det, mit Lohse dagegen später schon. Bills Selbst-
promotion als Genie war mir etwas zu viel, obwohl
ich seine Leistung, die von ihm angestrebte Einheit
der Gestaltung, sehr bewunderte. Ich hörte 1953 seinen Vortrag mit der Parole «Vom Löffel bis zur
Stadt» zur Eröffnung der Hochschule für Gestaltung
in Ulm und war beeindruckt davon, dass jemand das
Bauhaus wieder ins Leben rufen wollte.

<sup>TH</sup>     Lohse war etwas älter als wir, bereits ein
arrivierter Künstler, und so gab es ein gewisses kol-

legiales Gefälle. Er war nicht immer einverstanden mit dem, was wir taten, aber im Grunde genommen schätzte er Robert; sie führten freundschaftliche Streitgespräche. 1980 reisten wir zusammen mit Lohse an die erste Architektur-Biennale in Venedig, und dort sagte er uns, er müsse Robert die Freundschaft aufkündigen, denn unsere Ideen für das erwähnte Stoffdesign gingen nun wirklich zu weit. Natürlich war das mit der Freundschaft nicht ganz ernst gemeint, aber die Aussage zu den Stoffen schon.

RH    Da war schliesslich noch Camille Graeser, der mir am meisten entsprach, ein feinfühliger, gescheiter, nicht lauter und nicht übertrieben ehrgeiziger, aber substanzieller Mensch.

DS    Auf den Giedion-Kreis folgte der 1954 gegründete Club Bel Etage, für kurze Zeit an der Schifflände, dann über dem Restaurant Weisses Kreuz an der Falkenstrasse.

RH    Ich war Gründungsmitglied des Club Bel Etage, denn es gefiel mir, dass in einer Wohnung Ausstellungen gezeigt wurden, ohne dass es eine Galerie war. Dort lernte ich Meret Oppenheim kennen, die ihre künstlerische Arbeit eben wieder aufgenommen hatte; etwas später kaufte ich von ihr eine Zeichnung. Gegründet und betrieben wurde der Club von Gottfried Honegger, massgeblich aber

auch von seiner damaligen Frau Warja Lavater. Sammler gab es in diesem Club eigentlich nicht, Kunst zu kaufen war finanziell unerreichbar. Dafür war es wieder eine Art Salon, in dem man sich traf.

Das Berner Pendant zur Bel Etage war das Café Commerce an der Gerechtigkeitsgasse, wo alle verkehrten – von den Architekten des Atelier 5 über Teo Jakob mit seinem Möbelgeschäft bis zu den Künstler:innen. Ich kannte diesen Kreis über meine Tätigkeit als Möbelentwerfer.

DS    Welches war das erste Bild, das Sie gekauft haben?

RH    Ein kleines Bild von Emanuel Jacob, den ich im Club Bel Etage kennengelernt hatte. Zum damaligen Umfeld gehörte das Restaurant Kronenhalle, das noch sehr bescheiden war, der Künstlermaskenball, dann auch die Buchhandlungen; allerdings waren die Schriftsteller im Club nicht sehr präsent.

DS    Und was war Ihr erster Bilderkauf?

TH    Das Bild von Rupprecht Geiger, das ich bei Toni Gerber in Bern kaufen wollte, das er mir dann aber schenkte. Die strahlenden Farben, die Geiger verwendete, zogen mich an; Jahre später kamen noch Grafiken von Geiger dazu. Robert kaufte ein Bild von Georg Karl Pfahler, als er ab 1986 an der

Staatlichen Akademie der Bildenden Künste in Stuttgart unterrichtete.

Ich war während meiner Studienzeit mit Gerber, der in Bern erst in seiner Wohnung, dann in seiner Galerie Kunst ausstellte, sehr befreundet und lernte die Berner Künstler:innen kennen. Gerber stellte meine Skulpturen aus, denn ich fertigte damals unter dem Einfluss von Linck Mobiles an. Eine Zeit lang dachte ich sogar, ich würde in Richtung Kunst gehen, und stellte bei einem Schlosser meine Metallarbeiten selbst her. Als ich das Studium an der ETH 1964 abgeschlossen hatte, bewarb ich mich für das Eidgenössische Kunststipendium. Max Bill war in der Jury, und er sagte mir, meine Arbeiten seien recht gut, aber er habe meine Diplomarbeit an der ETH gesehen, und nach seiner Meinung sei ich auf diesem Gebiet begabter. Das war, als ich an der Expo 64 in Lausanne im Bau von Ernst Gisel eine grosse Spirale aufstellen konnte.

RH        Als mein Vater 1955 gestorben war, eröffnete ich mit meinem Bruder an der Oberdorfstrasse ein eigenes Geschäft, denn ich wollte weg von Stilmöbeln und Tapeten. In den Hinterräumen des Ladens hatte ich meinen Zeichnungstisch, an dem ich an Innenarchitekturaufgaben arbeitete. Meine Möbel wurden im Laden verkauft, doch zu Beginn gab es noch gar nicht viele davon. Daraus ergaben sich zahlreiche Kontakte.

Von den Künstler:innen, die damals eine Rolle spielten, kommt mir Varlin in den Sinn, von dem ich nur ein Bild besitze, obwohl er ein enger Freund war. Varlin wollte ein Doppelporträt von mir und meinem Bruder malen, denn wir hatten beide rote Haare. Um diese Zeit hatte er das Bild seiner späteren Frau Franca im Ozelotmantel fertiggestellt. Das Muster des Raubtierfells dominierte darin alles, und Varlin hatte die Idee, dass er es mit unseren roten Haaren ähnlich halten könnte. Ich bot ihm an, dafür einen Stoff in dieser Farbe zu besorgen. Varlin glaubte, dass in einem Doppelporträt immer einer der Dargestellten schlechter wegkomme. So schlug ich ihm vor, «Willy, mach doch zwei Leinwände, dann kannst Du sie nachher zusammenschieben». Er ging darauf ein, und ich besorgte bei Racher die Rahmen und marschierte damit zum Atelier am Neumarkt. Erst musste der eine von uns posieren, dann der andere; Varlin rief jeweils an, wenn er wieder einen benötigte. Dabei realisierte ich, dass das Posieren ebenso anstrengend wie die Arbeit des Malers ist. Wenn ich eine andere Jacke trug, wurde ich beschimpft, denn dann musste er das ganze Bild ummalen. Ich besitze das Doppelporträt jedoch nicht, denn erstens war das Format zu hoch, und wir hatten keinen Platz dafür; zweitens war es mir peinlich, hinter mir mein Bildnis an der Wand zu haben.

Um Varlin gab es am Rindermarkt in Zürich einen besonderen Kreis; dazu gehörten so verschiedenartige Künstler:innen wie Leo Leuppi, Colette Ryter, die nach Entwürfen von Jean Lurçat Teppiche wob, und Henry Wabel. Sie trafen sich am späten Vormittag zum Apéritif im Klosterbräu, und manchmal dauerte dies bis Mitternacht.

DS    Und der Kreis um Friedrich Kuhn?

RH    Das erste Bild von Kuhn kaufte ich an einer Weihnachtsausstellung im Helmhaus. Dann kam er immer wieder zu mir, wenn er blank war. Ich gab ihm etwas Geld und sagte, er solle mir auch etwas dafür geben, und so kam ich zu so vielen Bildern von ihm.

TH    Solche Bohème-Künstler hatte ich zuvor kaum kennengelernt. Zwar schätzte ich die Bilder von Friedrich Kuhn, aber seine überschäumende Art befremdete mich etwas. Auch Dieter Roth war so, er machte stets etwas Unerwartetes. Dafür haben wir schöne Erinnerungen an Hanny Fries; sie war eine gute Freundin.

RH    Die 1953 von Ernst Gisel entworfenen Ateliers an der Wuhrstrasse in Zürich waren etwas Ausserordentliches. Gisel setzte sich mit dem Maler Max Truninger dafür ein, dass Ateliers für Künstler:innen gebaut werden konnten; sie suchten dafür Geld bei

Firmen und waren erfolgreich. Neben Friedrich Kuhn hatten Muz Zeier, Trudi Demut und Otto Müller dort ihre Ateliers.

TH      Otto Müller und Trudi Demut waren enge Freunde von uns. Trudi Demut hatte, einmal abgesehen von ihren Plastiken, die Fähigkeit, aus allem, auch aus ihrer einfachen Wohnung, etwas Schönes zu arrangieren. Sie schenkte uns Bronzemaquetten ihrer wichtigen Arbeiten; in diesen oft sehr feinen Arbeiten kommt ihre Sensibilität am stärksten zum Ausdruck. Wir erwarben von ihr einen grossen Gips und zwei Bilder.

RH      Bei Otto Müller beeindruckte mich die Reduktion eines Gegenstandes auf immer einfachere Formen; besonders tritt dies an seinen Köpfen hervor, von denen er richtig besessen war.

TH      Ähnlich ist es bei seinem Bronzerelief *Frau Welt*, die keine Frau mehr ist, sondern durch das Weglassen von Details zu einer starken, expressiven Figur wird.

RH      Wir haben von ihm neben Plastiken eine grosse und mehrere kleine Zeichnungen. Es gelang mir ein paar Male, Otto einen Auftrag zu vermitteln, so beispielsweise 1979 im alten Botanischen Garten in Zürich, wo wir mit den Architekt:innen Hans und

Annemarie Hubacher die bestehenden Gebäude in das Völkerkundemuseum umbauten, und 2001 für den Innenhof des Bürohauses im Heiligkreuz von Toni Bargetze in Vaduz, dessen Inneres wir gestalteten.

Ich nahm Otto und Trudi einmal auf eine Reise nach Frankreich mit, und es war eine schöne Erfahrung, gemeinsam mit diesen beiden Menschen Bauten zu entdecken und zu sehen. Trudi hielt alles in ihrem Tagebuch fest. Le Corbusiers Notre-Dame-du-Haut in Ronchamp sah ich erstmals auf dieser Reise.

Alle diese Künstler:innen waren sehr differenzierte Menschen, mit denen man sich traf, mit denen man diskutierte, was in der Kunst vor sich ging, und auch stritt. Otto Müller, Hans Aeschbacher, Heinrich Eichmann und Hans Fischli waren alle plastisch tätig – befreundet, befeindet, entfreundet …

DS    In Zürich gab es seit den 1960er-Jahren einige Galerien, die für die Vermittlung internationaler neuer Kunst Wichtiges leisteten.

RH    Wir besuchten regelmässig Bruno Bischofberger, Renée und Maurice Ziegler, Gimpel & Hanover und Pierre Baltensperger. Da ich mit Willy Rotzlers Frau Anne und mit Erika Brausen in London befreundet war, war ich mit Rat und Tat dabei, als die Galerie Gimpel & Hanover 1962 neue Räume an der Claridenstrasse in Zürich bezog. Das war kein eigentliches Projekt, ich machte einfach Vorschläge,

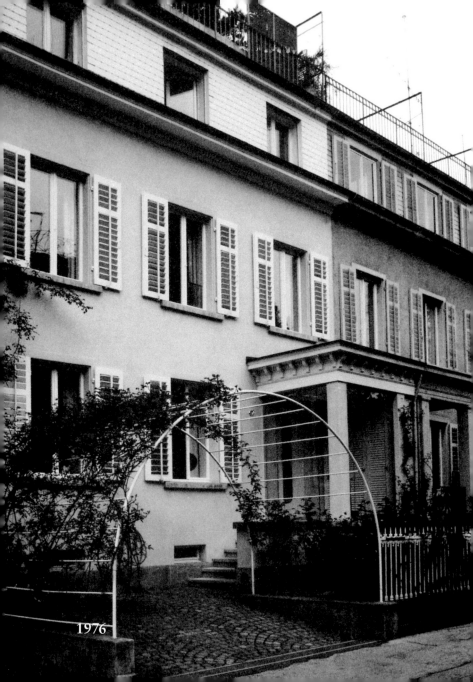

1976

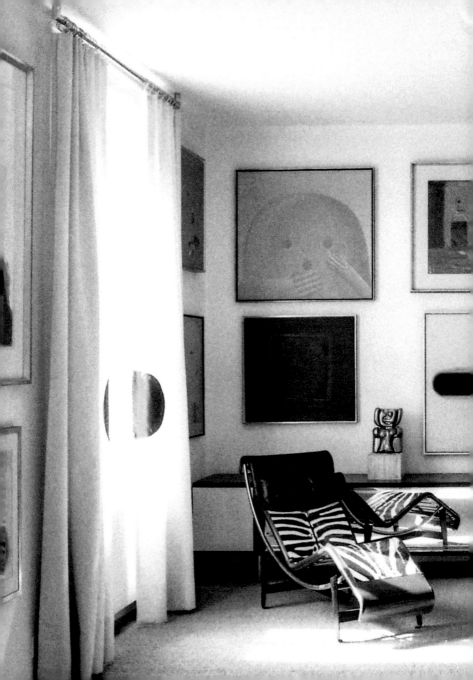

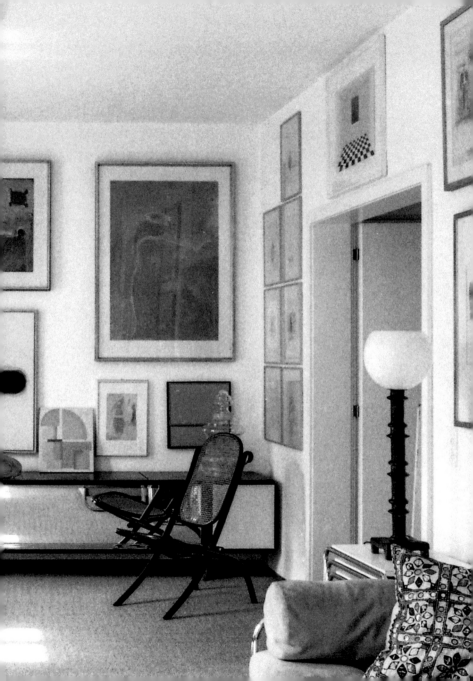

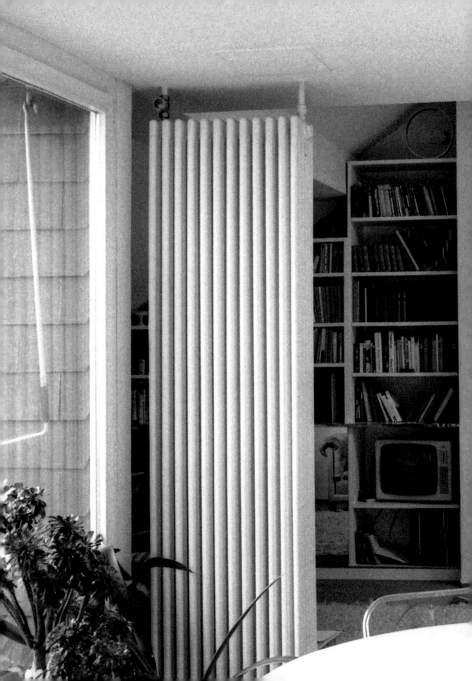

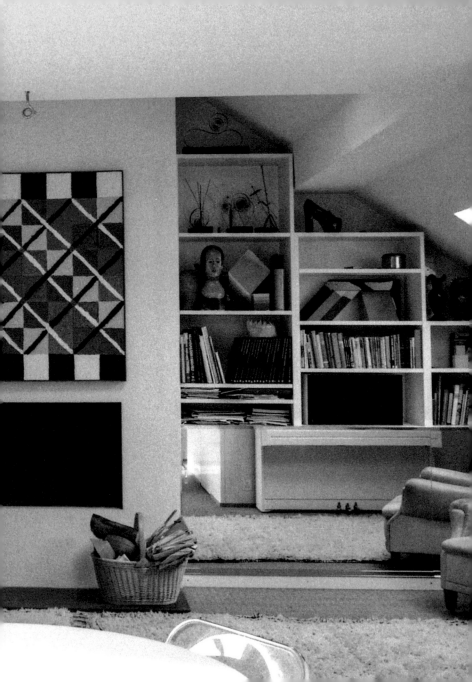

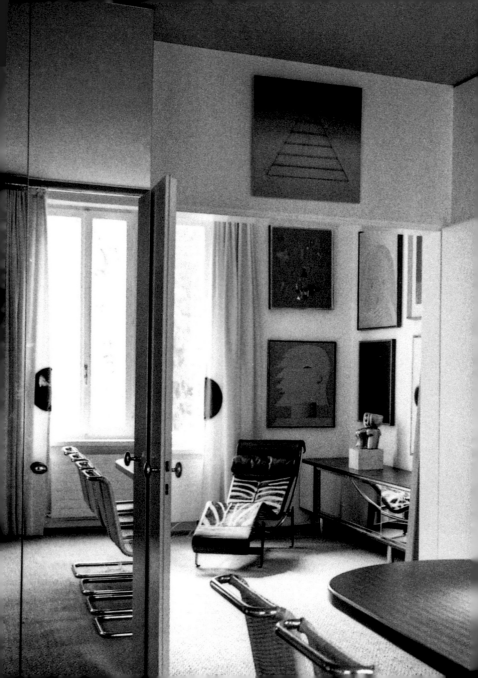

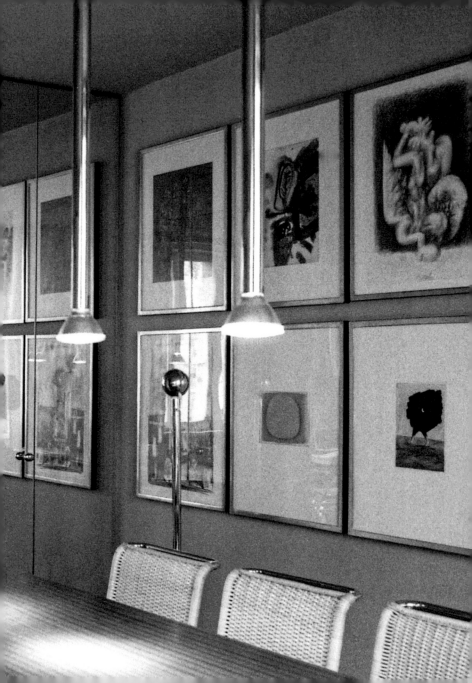

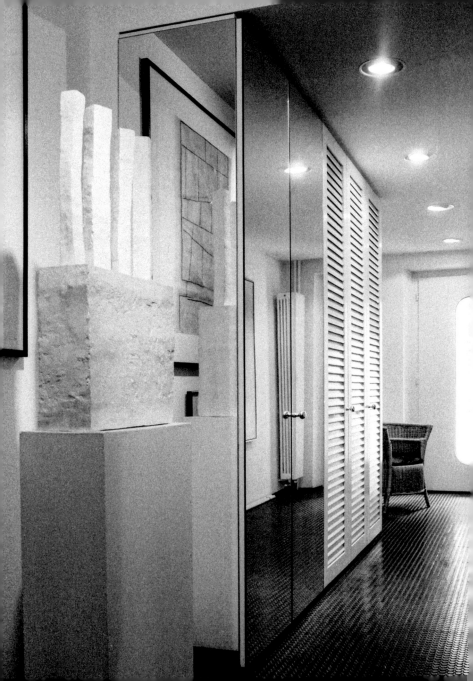

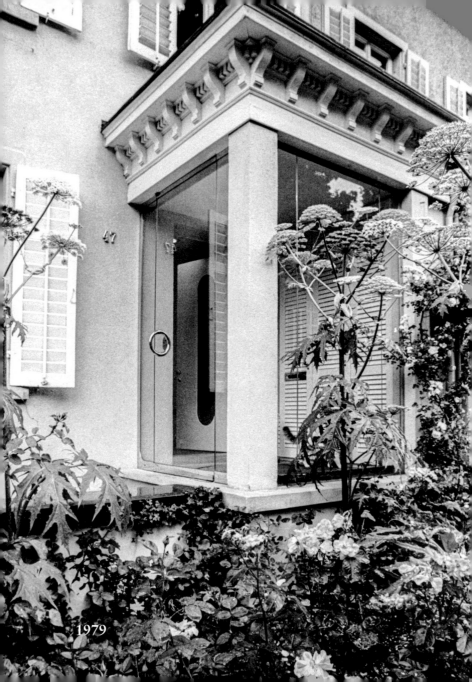

1979

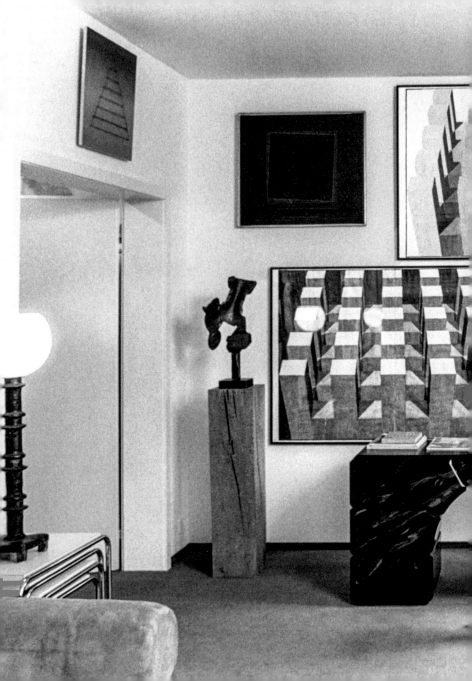

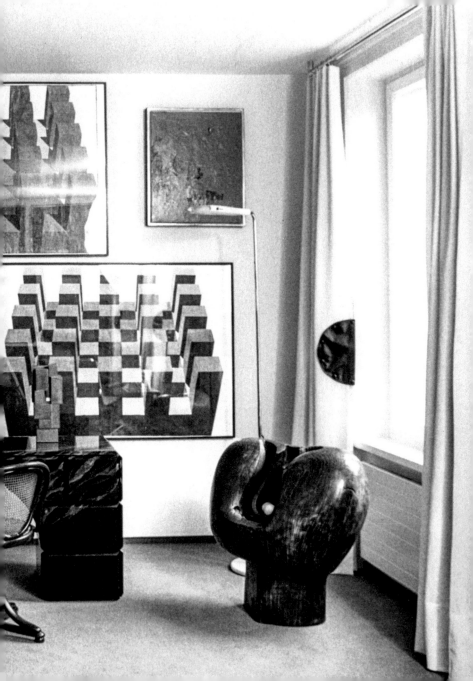

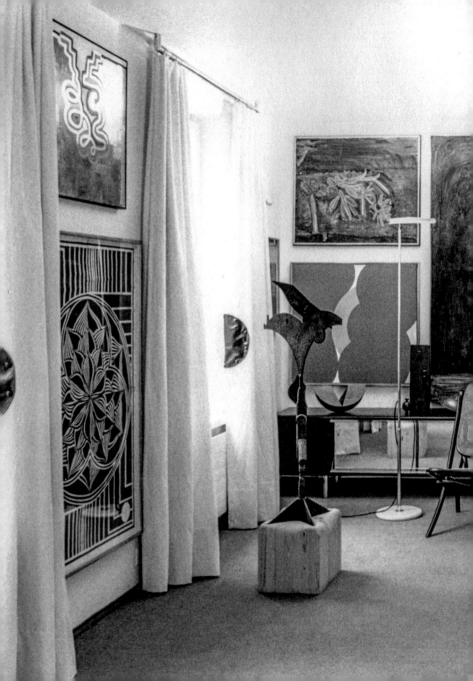

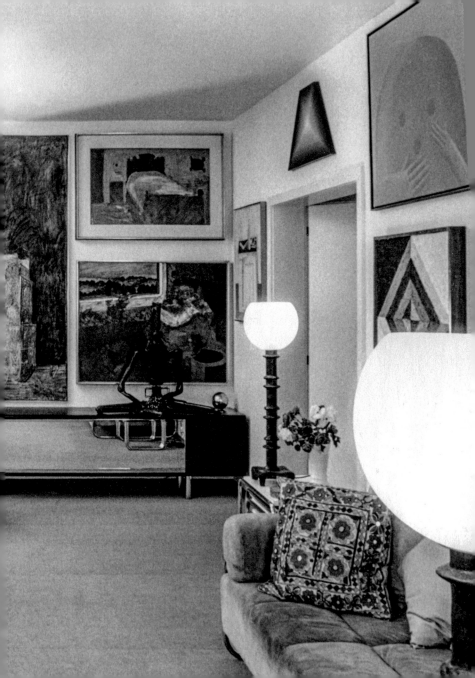

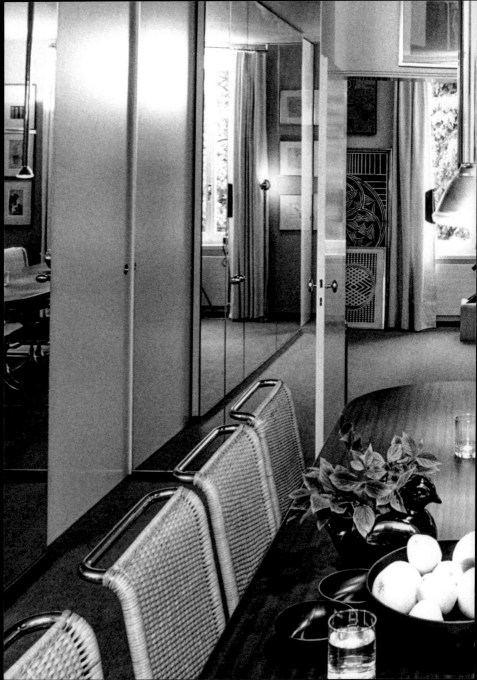

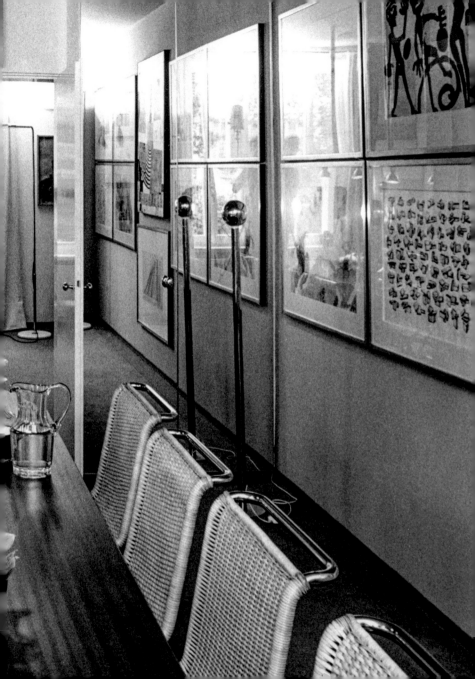

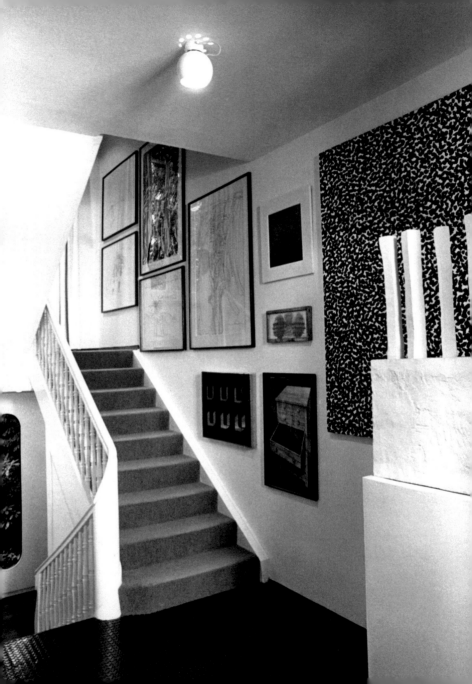

wie man die Räume besser nutzen könnte. So stellte sich beispielsweise die Frage, wie man mit dem ehemaligen Ladenraum mit einem grossen Schaufenster und ohne Lager umgeht. Ich entwickelte bewegliche raumhohe Ausstellungswände, die man vor die Wände schob, damit man dahinter nicht sichtbar Bilder hängen konnte. Die Bildträger für die Ausstellungen dienten zugleich als Verblendung der realen Wände. Manchmal begleitete ich auch die Gestaltung von Ausstellungen, aber nicht mit baulichen Massnahmen.

DS      Ein wichtiges Projekt war 1968 die Gestaltung der Räume für die Galerie Maeght in Zürich.

RH      Der Kontakt zu Aimé und Marguerite Maeght in Paris kam durch den Zürcher Seidenhändler und Kunstsammler Gustav Zumsteg zustande. Erst erhielt ich 1967 den Auftrag für den Umbau der Galerie Maeght an der Rue de Téhéran in Paris. Aus der Blechverkleidung der Galeriefassade im Gebäudesockel wurde allerdings nichts; das Projekt versandete aus mir nicht bekannten Gründen. In Zürich begann es damit, dass mein Bruder ein Haus am Predigerplatz kaufte, das man gänzlich renovieren und umbauen musste. Wir arbeiteten mit der Denkmalpflege zusammen und gestalteten Sandsteinumrandungen für die Fenster, doch es zeigte sich schliesslich, dass die vermeintlich historische Fassade gar nicht aus Sandstein, sondern bloss aus Blech

war. Für die im Erdgeschoss gelegene Galerie schufen wir einen neuen, unterirdischen Raum, um einen Rundgang herzustellen: Man betrat die Galerie, ging dann die Treppe hinunter in den lang gezogenen Raum, stieg in einen kleineren Raum empor und kam durch den Innenhof wieder zum Eingang zurück.

DS   Durch die wechselnden Raumsituationen entstand eine wirkungsvolle, immer wieder überraschende Dramaturgie für die Ausstellungen. Die schmalen Räume auf zwei Ebenen hatten einen eigenen Charme, besonders der von hohen Mauern umgebene Innenhof, in dem Skulpturen standen.

Nun aber wieder zurück zur Sammlung. Die deutschen Maler Horst Antes, Geiger und Pfahler, der Belgier Bram Bogart und Alfred Jensen, fallen als internationale Künstler etwas aus der Sammlung heraus, die sonst meist Schweizer Künstler:innen umfasst. Die internationalen Künstler:innen standen ausserhalb Ihres Bekanntenkreises, wurden aber von Schweizer Galerien wie Ziegler und Kornfeld in Bern vermittelt.

RH   Jensen war eine ausserordentliche Erscheinung, die sich von allem unterschied, was wir kannten.

TH   Ich kannte Jensen aus Bern, da Adolf Max Vogts Bruder, Werner Vogt, bei Kornfeld drei grosse Bilder gekauft hatte, die mich beeindruckten.

DS     War es vielleicht auch die Tatsache, dass Jensen kein konstruktiver Künstler im Sinne der Zürcher Konkreten war, sondern dass man an ihm etwas Manieristisches entdecken konnte, die Synthese von Zahlenordnungen der Maya und der griechischen Antike?

TH     Mit seiner Zahlenmystik hatte Jensen etwas Esoterisches, das uns faszinierte.

RH     Es war wie eine eigene Religion, es ging davon eine starke Kraft aus. Jensens Arbeit mit Gitterquadraten regte mich dazu an, selbst herauszufinden, was in einem quadrierten Zeichenblock steckt – vom Trompe-l'œil bis zur Konstruktion liegt alles darin.

DS     Die Gestaltung der Kronenhalle-Bar im Jahre 1965 war Anlass zur Zusammenarbeit mit Alberto und Diego Giacometti.

RH     Es begann damit, dass Gustav Zumsteg mich ansprach und fragte, ob ich Zeit hätte, etwas zu besprechen. Er tat sehr geheimnisvoll, seine Mutter Hulda Zumsteg, die Wirtin der Kronenhalle, dürfe dies nicht wissen. An einem Sonntagnachmittag teilte er mir mit, dass er im Coiffeur-Salon neben der Kronenhalle eine Bar einrichten möchte. Dieser Salon war übrigens auch aus Mahagoni … Er fragte

mich, ob ich diese Aufgabe übernehmen würde, und
ich hatte auch gleich Ideen, wie eine schöne Bar aus-
sehen könnte. Beim nächsten Treffen kamen wir
beide mit Publikationen über Adolf Loos' Kärntner
Bar an – es ist selten, dass Bauherr und Architekt
dieselbe Vorstellung von einem Projekt haben.

TH      Ihr spracht über das Licht, und du sagtest,
dass du die Lampen immer selbst gezeichnet habest;
aber nun dachtest du an jemanden, der dies besonders gut könnte.

RH      Ich erzählte Zumsteg von meiner Begeiste-
rung für die Lampen von Alberto und Diego Giacometti aus den 1930er-Jahren, als sie für den Pariser
Möbeldesigner Jean-Michel Frank dekorative Ge-
genstände entwarfen. Ich kannte diese Lampen nur
aus Büchern, hatte sie nie wirklich gesehen. Zumsteg
sagte, die beiden seien Freunde von ihm, und ob ich
am kommenden Mittwoch nicht Zeit hätte, mit ihm
nach Paris zu fahren. Wir trafen dort Diego, und ich
arbeitete eigentlich ausschliesslich mit ihm. Alberto
war nur einmal dabei, als die beiden Brüder nach
Zürich kamen und mir die Lampen vorführten. Ich
hatte ein Sperrholzmodell vorbereitet, damit man
sehen konnte, wie hoch die Bar war, und auch für
die Stühle gab es einen Prototypen. Das Gipsmodell,
das sie mitbrachten, hatte billige Glaskugeln. Ich
schlug Alabaster vor, weil dieses Material mit Bron-

ze kombiniert sehr schön wirkt, und sie waren davon begeistert.

DS    Beschäftigte sich hauptsächlich Diego mit diesem Projekt? Er führte ja auch die Bronzen für Alberto aus.

RH    Ja, die Ausführung lag in seinen Händen.

DS    Mich erstaunt, dass Alberto sich in dieser Lebensphase, zur Zeit der Bildnisbüsten von Elie Lotar, nochmals mit einem dekorativen Projekt befasste.

RH    Das kam durch die Freundschaft mit Zumsteg – ein unwahrscheinlicher Glücksfall. Alberto hatte das kleine Atelier mit der *soupente*, und daneben hatte Diego seine Werkstatt, eine Art Schlosserei. Alberto arbeitete mit Gips auf Armaturen, die Diego für ihn vorbereitet hatte. Diego spürte, was Alberto brauchte, er war klar der Helfer. Die beiden Brüder hatten eine ganz eigene Art, miteinander zu reden; sie lebten in einer Symbiose.

DS    Ging der Kontakt mit Diego nach Albertos Tod weiter?

RH    Ja, Diego rettete mich sogar einmal! Wir waren von Zumsteg zu einer Pariser Modenschau mit

Grand Dîner eingeladen, und ich fühlte mich dort sehr fehl am Platz. Diego war auch anwesend, und ich sah von weitem, dass er sich ebenso unwohl fühlte. Da passierte mir ein Missgeschick: Als ich eine Zigarette anzünden wollte, entzündete sich das Streichholzbriefchen in meiner rechten Hand, und ich erlitt starke Verbrennungen. Diego stürzte auf mich zu, führte uns hinaus und brachte uns in seine Werkstatt. Dort verband er mich fachmännisch, und wir waren von seinem Geschick tief beeindruckt.

Mehrmals trafen wir uns in Paris im Café Les Deux Magots. Dort beschloss man jeweils, zu Lipp zum Abendessen zu gehen, doch Lipp war jedesmal voll, und man musste anderswohin – es war stets dasselbe Ritual.

DS    Aber in Ihrer Sammlung sind die Brüder nicht vertreten?

TH    Doch, es gibt zwei Alabasterlampen von Diego. Wir hätten auch gern einen Tisch gehabt, und Diego notierte unsere Bestellung, doch jedesmal, wenn wir nach Paris kamen, war uns gerade jemand zuvorgekommen, der den Tisch gekauft hatte. Die grossen Sammler aus der Zürcher Gesellschaft kamen eben zuerst dran …

RH    Für eine Arbeit von Alberto war es zu spät. Eine Zeit lang hatten wir von Gimpel & Hanover

eine sitzende Figur in Bronze hier zur Ansicht, doch war sie bereits zu teuer für uns.

TH     Es geschah immer wieder, dass wir gern etwas von jemandem gehabt hätten, den wir gut kannten, und dennoch kam es nicht dazu.

DS     Wir haben von der Zusammenarbeit mit den Brüdern Giacometti gesprochen. Gab es noch andere Projekte mit Künstler:innen?

RH     Als Heinrich Eichmann 1965 im neuen Stadttheater Ingolstadt ein grosses Wandbild realisieren konnte, holte er mich für die Inneinrichtung und empfahl mich für die Beleuchtung. Eichmann war von Beruf Flachmaler; er hatte in den 1930er-Jahren zu den Spanien-Kämpfern gehört und engagierte sich später politisch als Leiter der Gipser- und Malergenossenschaft in Zürich. Er stand in der Nachkriegszeit den Zürcher Konkreten nahe, und nach seiner Pensionierung wandte er sich erneut der Kunst zu und malte ornamentale Tafelbilder mit Blattgold. Diese Technik war etwas Besonderes. In Ingolstadt konnte er auf der Sichtbetonwand grosse Wandreliefs mit Blattgold ausführen, was etwas gänzlich Neues war.

TH     Als wir 1970 das Innere des Hallenbades im Hotel Mont Cervin in Zermatt gestalteten, hatten

wir Eichmann für ein Wandbild engagiert. Der Auftraggeber versuchte anschliessend, Eichmanns Honorar zu drücken, doch dieser antwortete: «Wissen Sie, ich als Künstler bin näher bei Gott als Sie.»

RH     Den Künstler Max Wiederkehr kannte ich von der Kunstgewerbeschule, wo er als Bauzeichner hinkam. Von ihm kaufte ich zahlreiche Zeichnungen, wenn er Geld brauchte. Wiederkehr lebte in Zürich, reiste in den 1960er-Jahren nach Indien und bewegte sich in einer esoterischen Welt, zu der ich eher Distanz hatte; er stellte kaum aus, war ein Aussenseiter. Eine Zeit lang war er bei mir angestellt, erschien zur Arbeit, wenn es ihm passte, und tauchte wieder ab. Sein Werk ist ziemlich heterogen: Es gibt Zeichnungen mit Pop-Figuren, dann wieder Tafeln mit Mandalas und geometrischen Elementen; in seinen späten Werken befasste er sich mit Zahlenordnungen. Ich nahm Max Wiederkehr unter meine Fittiche und brachte es zustande, dass er in Ingolstadt ein Relief für das Theaterrestaurant machen konnte.

TH     Gemeinsam mit Markus Raetz nahmen wir 1968 am Wettbewerb für den Schweizer Pavillon an der Expo '70 in Osaka teil. Ich hatte Markus in meiner Berner Zeit kennengelernt und hatte damals eine eigene Kleinplastik gegen ein kleines Relief von ihm getauscht. Dann kauften wir das Relief *Goppenstein*, das rosafarbene Eisenbahnfenster mit den

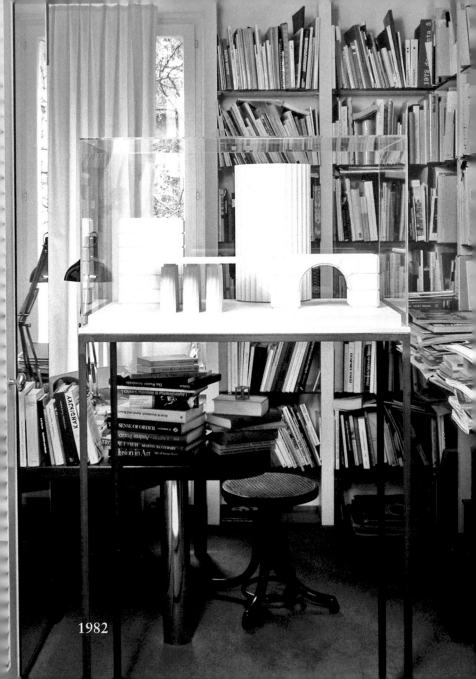

1982

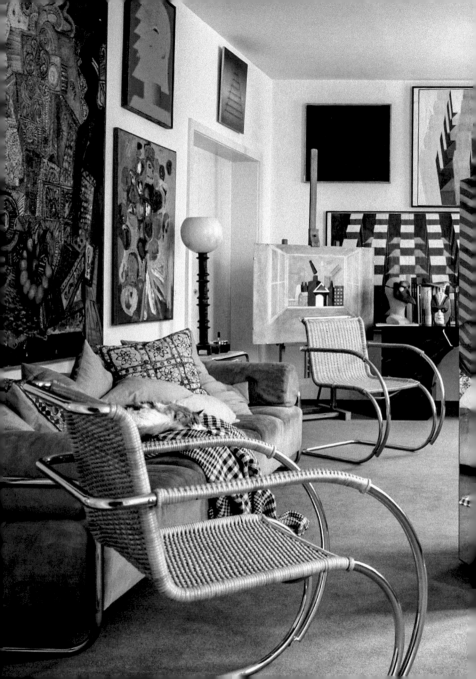

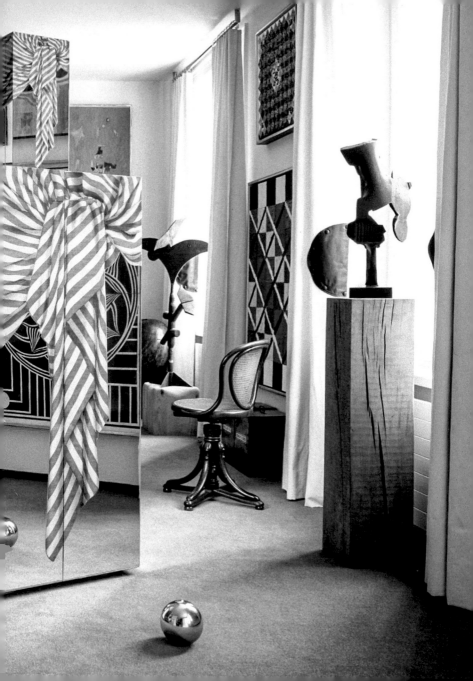

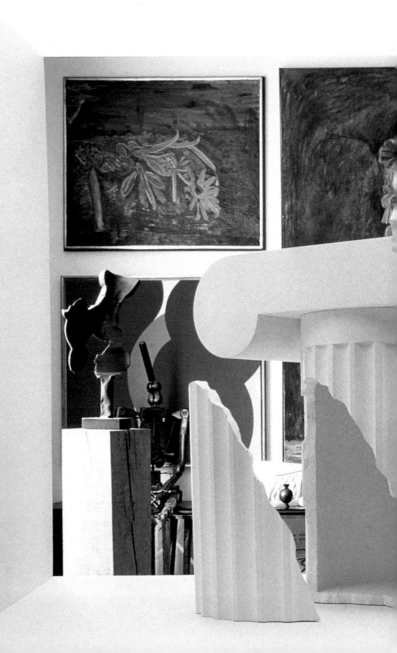

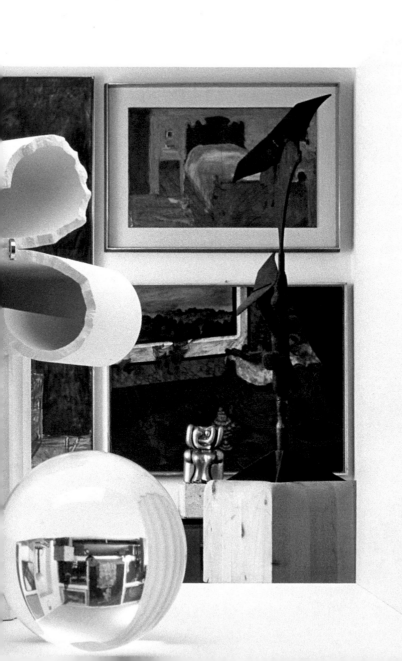

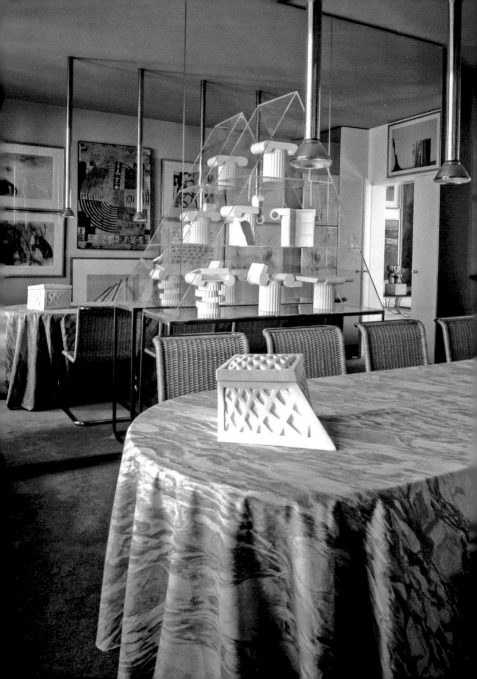

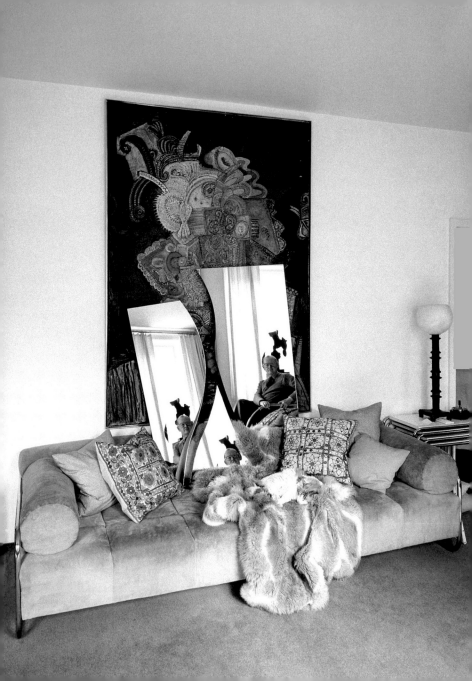

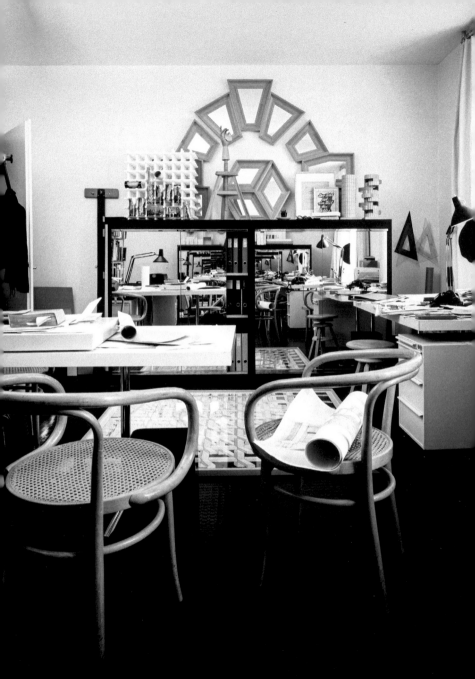

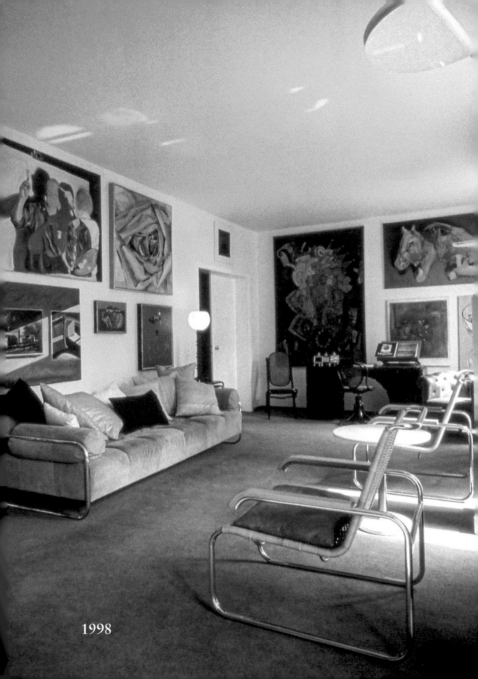

1998

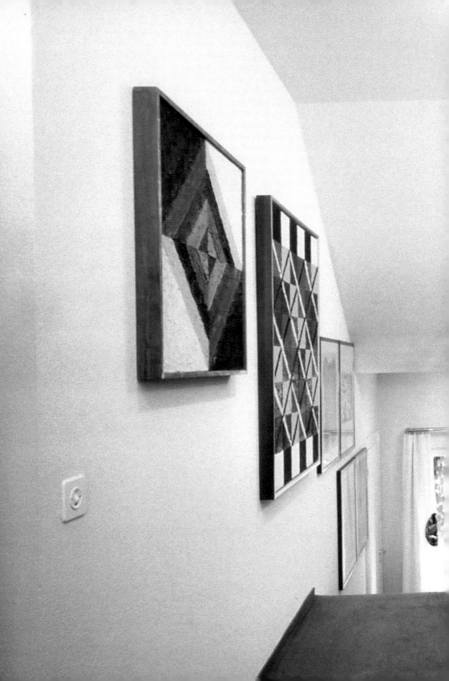

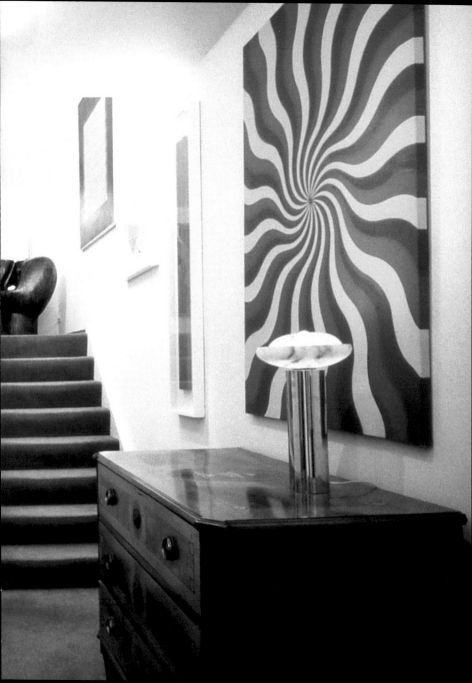

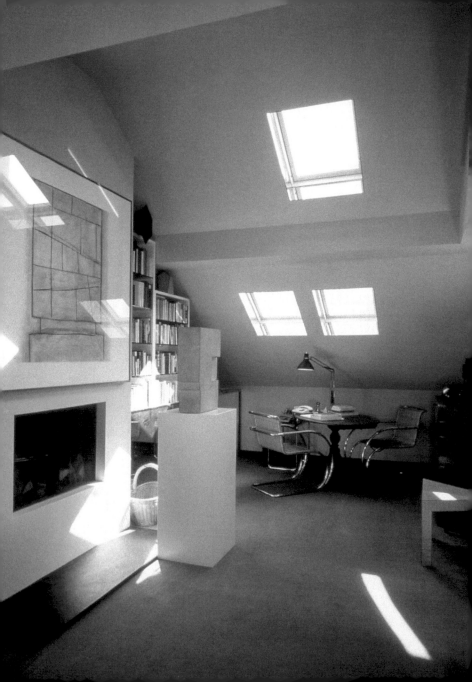

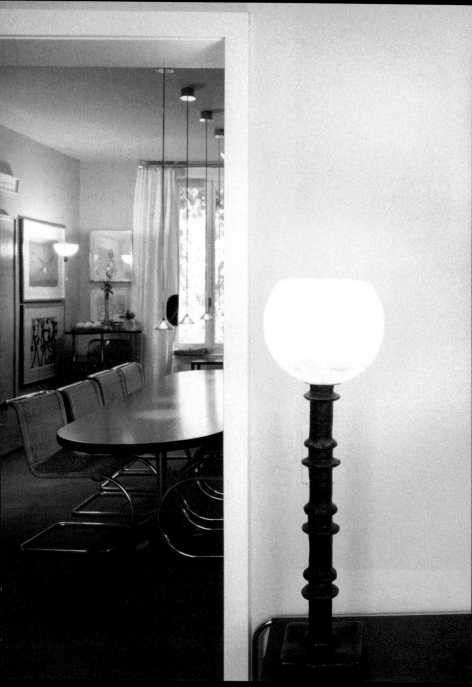

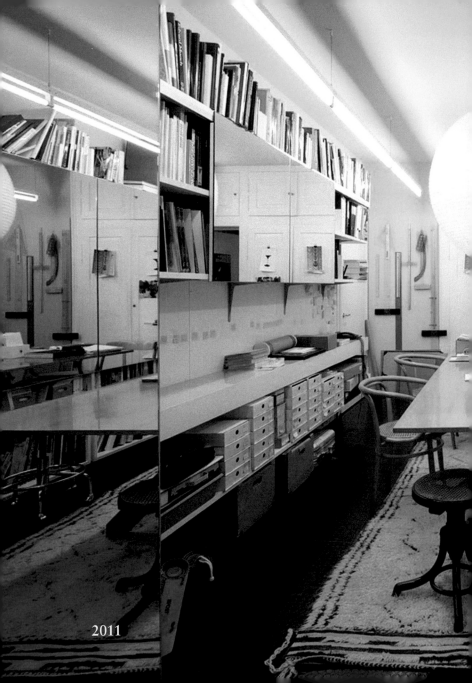

2011

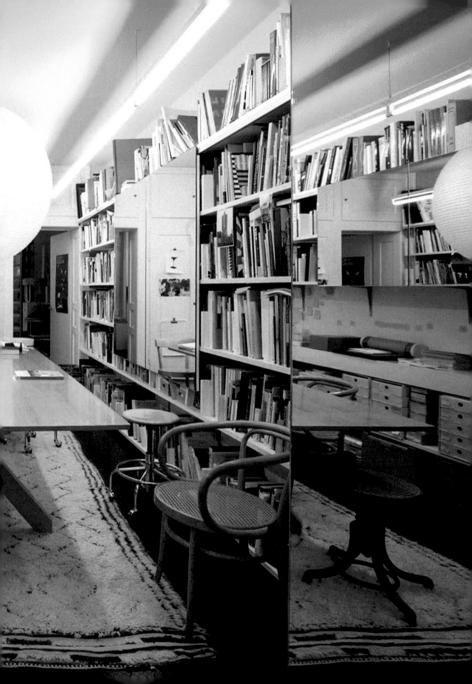

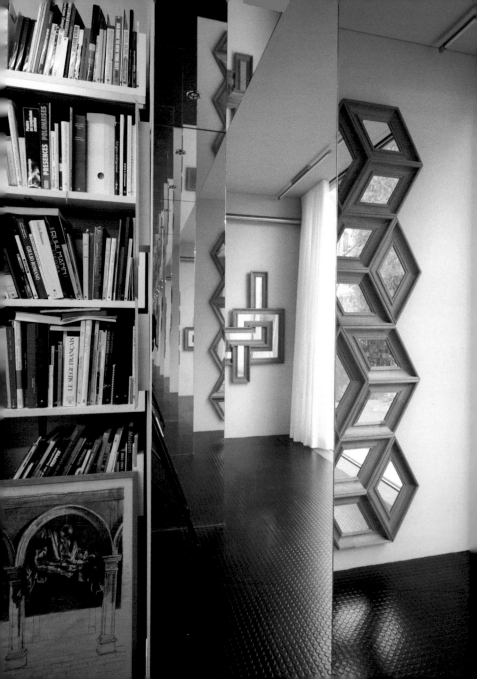

ausgesparten Wölkchen, die daneben auf der Wand schweben. Das war die Inspiration für unseren Vorschlag an Markus, für den Wettbewerb einen Koffer für eine Wolke zu entwerfen.

RH    Und so zeichnete er einen detaillierten Plan mit den vielfältigen Eigenschaften dieses Koffers, doch leider kamen wir nicht in die Ränge.

TH    In letzter Zeit arbeiteten wir mit Daniel Sommer, der am Institut gta der ETH die Ausstellungen gestaltet und eigene graphische Arbeiten macht. Er machte 2020 an der Entwicklung der grossen Spiegelskulptur *Enigma* für die Biennale «Sculpture Garden» in Genf mit.

DS    Ich möchte zurückkommen auf das Programm des «Manierismo critico», wie Sie es nannten. 1981 schrieben Sie im Zusammenhang mit der Ausstellung Ihrer Arbeiten im Studio Marconi in Mailand einen Aufsatz für die Zeitschrift *Werk, Bauen + Wohnen* (Nr. 10, 1981) und sprachen von der «Suche nach anderen Ausdrucksmöglichkeiten» und dem «wachsenden Zweifel an manchen Dogmen der Moderne». Sie entwarfen ein Programm, das Gestaltungsmittel wie die Materialverfremdung, das Schaffen von illusionärem Raum durch Spiegelung, die illusionistische Körper- und Raumveränderung, die Verwendung literarischer Formen, die Mehrdeu-

tigkeit, den Einbezug von Widerspruch, Störung und Zerstörung umfasste. Waren diese Gedanken auch programmatisch für Ihre Annäherung an die Kunst? Haben sie Ihr Kunstverständnis geprägt?

TH       Wir waren geprägt von der klassischen Moderne, zu der unsere Lehrer gehörten, und setzten uns nun historisch mit dem Phänomen Manierismus auseinander, denn wir gewannen den Eindruck, dass man in den 1980er-Jahren in vieler Hinsicht einen manieristischen Umbruch erlebte. Unsere Sache waren nicht die Pflastersteine, wir fanden diesen Umbruch eher in der Kunst. Dann ging es uns auch darum, diese Phänomene als Lehrstücke genau zu beschreiben …

RH       … reduziert und konstruiert zu zeigen, zunächst anhand von Modellen. Wir realisierten, dass es für die sogenannte Postmoderne einen klareren Begriff brauchte, und so versuchte ich, dies sprachlich zu formulieren.

DS       Wenn man sich bei Ihnen umschaut, dann könnte man sagen, dass viele der Zeichnungen und Bilder, die hier hängen, Merkmale des «Manierismo critico» zeigen. Am stringentesten erfüllt wahrscheinlich André Thomkins in Ihrer Sammlung das kritisch-manieristische Programm.

RH Thomkins war ein sehr guter Freund. Wir lernten ihn 1969 an seiner Ausstellung bei Felix Handschin in Basel kennen, wahrscheinlich sogar schon zuvor durch Paul Gredinger und Markus Kutter von der Werbeagentur GGK, für die wir verschiedentlich gearbeitet hatten. Mir gefielen besonders seine Palindrome und Anagramme, der spielerische Umgang mit der Sprache.

DS Mit dem im Marconi-Katalog publizierten Begriffsschieber, der erlaubt, zwei beliebige Begriffe miteinander zu einer neuen Einheit zu kombinieren, haben Sie etwas Ähnliches erfunden.

TH Ich habe Roberts Sprachspiele gesammelt und zu seinem 75. Geburtstag in einem Büchlein unter dem Titel *Verlorene Eier – ein gefundenes Fressen* herausgegeben. Darin tritt deutlich sein sprachliches Interesse zutage, es dokumentiert aber auch die Zeit, als man im Kreis von Künstlern wie Thomkins und Daniel Spoerri ständig Wortspiele produzierte. Wir besitzen ein Fallenbild von Spoerri, das einmal von der Wand fiel, da es schlecht aufgehängt war. Wir klebten es notdürftig zusammen, aber vor allem stellten wir uns die Frage: Was machen wir mit einem gefallenen Fallenbild?

 Oft war Thomkins bei uns in Zürich zu Gast und verbrachte etwas Zeit hier, wenn er Distanz zu seiner Familie in Essen suchte.

<sup>DS</sup> Durch Thomkins lernten Sie Johannes Geuer aus Düsseldorf kennen?

<sup>TH</sup> Ja, und dann durch Geuers Ausstellung bei Galerie Stähli, Langenbacher + Wankmiller in Luzern. Aber bald zerstritt sich Geuer mit der Galerie wie später auch mit vielen anderen.

<sup>RH</sup> Mich faszinierte an Geuer das malerische Können, kombiniert mit seinen Ideen, wie beispielsweise im Bild nach Picassos *Villa Californie* oder in dem klassischen Intérieur, wo auf den Möbeln Schnee liegt ...

<sup>TH</sup> ... oder das Intérieur unter Wasser, das er in einem Aquarium einrichtete. Er sprühte vor Ideen und machte immer neue Erfindungen. Als er einmal ein paar Wochen in dem alten Bauernhaus auf dem Ibrig wohnte, unserem Ferienhaus, sah er die Ziegen auf der Wiese und beschloss, zusammen mit ihnen ein Bild zu malen. Er nahm dafür einen Papierbogen, verteilte die Farben darauf und streute Salz darüber. Die Ziegen kamen, leckten das Salz ab – sie bekamen farbige Zungen –, und so entstand das Bild.

Wenn Johannes bei uns wohnte, blieb er oft lange auf, zeichnete und trank, und am Morgen fand ich dann ein Blatt, auf das er gute Ratschläge für den Tag aufgeschrieben hatte, einmal zum Beispiel «Liebe Trix, heute nix».

RH Nahe war uns auch Anton Bruhin, dessen Vielseitigkeit – Maultrommelmusiker, Maler von figürlichen Bildern, Zeichner von Kalligrafien und Dichter – mir sehr gefiel. Für mich waren seine *Heldengesänge* in einer erfundenen Sprache, in einem pseudomittelalterlichen Duktus, besonders interessant. Er machte 2006 eine Ausstellung in einer Galerie unter dem Titel *Schöne Bilder!*

DS Er verfasste Palindrome, und das sind wiederum sprachliche Spiegel.

RH Gut gefällt mir das Bild des ehemaligen Bauhäuslers Xanti Schawinsky. Er benutzte für dieses Bild eine selbst erfundene Technik, indem er die Leinwand zerknüllte und dann mit der Spritzpistole bearbeitete, um auf diese Weise zufällige Effekte zu erzielen. Erwähnen möchte ich auch Hans Witschi, den ich für einen sehr guten Maler halte.

DS Der andere Schweizer Manierist, den man nennen könnte, ist Bernhard Luginbühl; nicht der junge, konstruktive und strenge Bildhauer mit seinen C-Formen, dafür der späte Luginbühl mit den Atlas-Kugeln und seiner Erzählfreudigkeit würde in diesen Kontext passen, im weiteren auch Jean Tinguely.

<sup>TH</sup> Vielleicht ist der Unterschied, wie viel Gedankenarbeit dahinter steckt; bei uns ist der Manierismus nicht bloss eine spontane Geste.

<sup>DS</sup> Wenn man den «Manierismo critico», Ihre Arbeit mit Studio Alchimia und die Kontakte zu Memphis bedenkt, dann hätten Sie sich auch der italienischen Kunst zuwenden können, denn da gab es von Giorgio de Chirico an aufwärts manches, was sich mit Ihren Gedanken vertragen hätte. Aber ich sehe bei Ihnen eigentlich nur das kleine Bild von Antonio Calderara.

<sup>RH</sup> Da ist noch ein schönes Bild von Aldo Rossi, auf dem prägende Elemente seiner Architektur vorkommen – die Säulen, der Giebel mit dem kreisförmigen Loch. Anlässlich der Architektur-Biennale von 1980 in Venedig baute er auf einem Schiff sein «Teatro del mondo» auf; das war ausserordentlich schön. Er, ebenso wie die Kolleg:innen vom Studio Alchimia, wussten selbst gar nicht, ob das nun Kunst sei, was sie produzierten, oder nicht.

<sup>TH</sup> Die letzte gemeinsame Aktion war der Plan für eine Ausstellung zum 40. Geburtstag von Alchimia unter dem Titel *L'uomo architetto*. Alessandro Guerriero, der Gründer von Alchimia, lud dazu die alten Kämpen ein. Die Bedingungen für die Beiträge waren streng – das Objekt durfte nicht höher als

35 Zentimeter sein –, und ein Termin wurde festgesetzt. Wir nahmen das sehr ernst, machten unser Objekt genau so gross und sandten es rechtzeitig ein, aber wir waren damit die Einzigen.

RH    Zum Teil waren die Ankäufe von Kunstwerken Zufälle; es ergab sich einfach. Wir haben ganz unsystematisch gekauft.

TH    Wir haben nie an eine Sammlungsstrategie geglaubt.

RH    Es ging um den Kontrast. Als Architekt:innen sind wir rationale Menschen, und das ist auch gut so. Manche von den Künstler:innen, die wir kannten, waren Aussenseiter, doch Architekt:innen als Aussenseiter – das gibt es eher weniger.

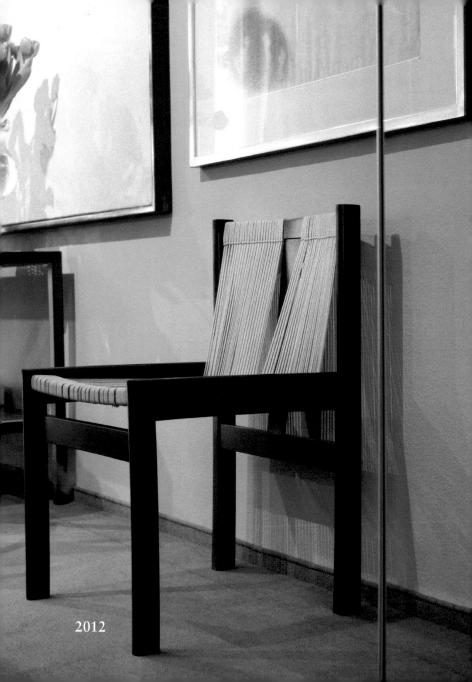

2012

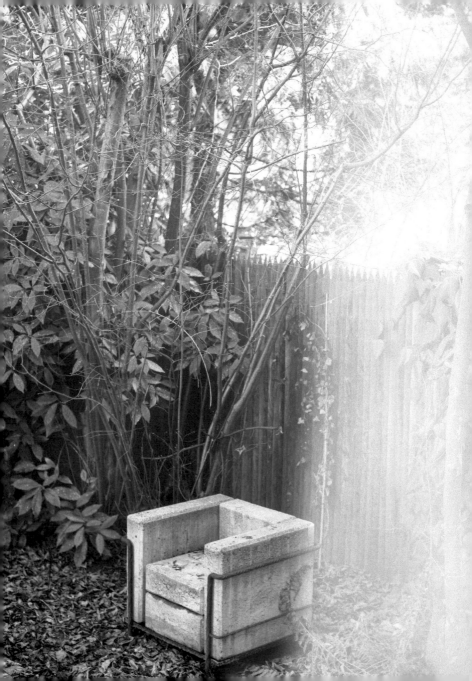

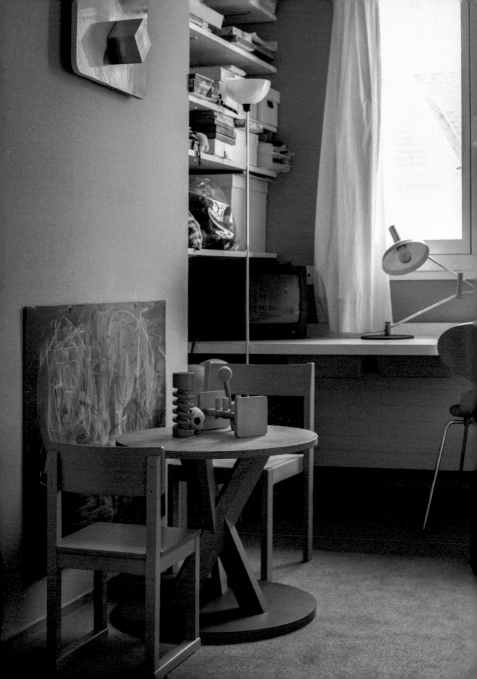

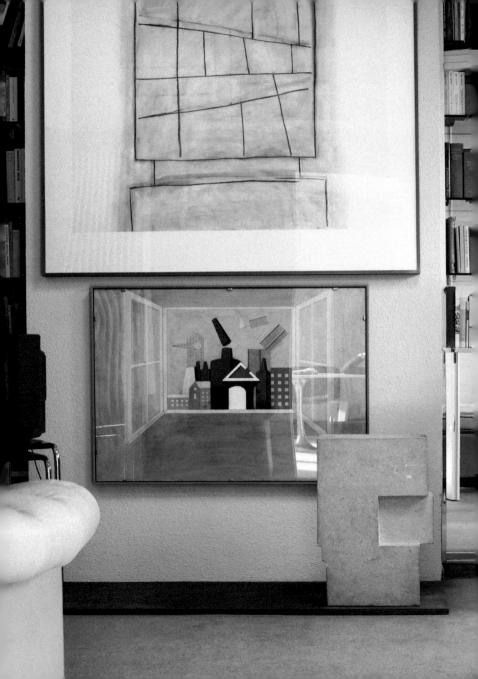

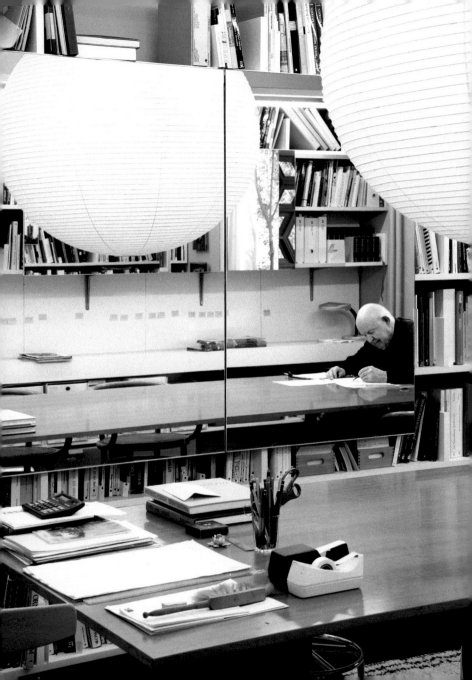

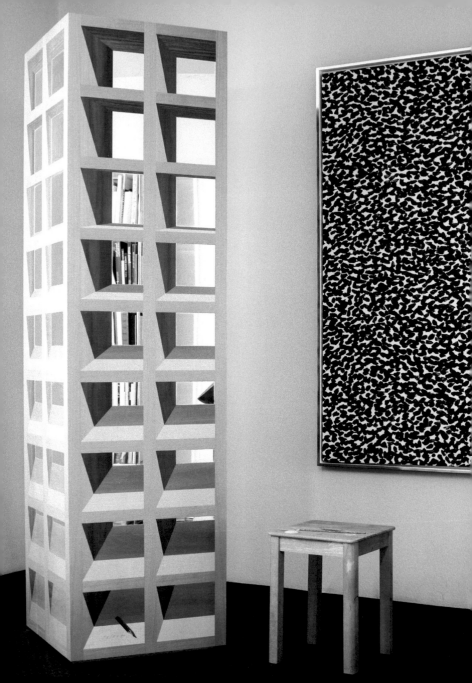

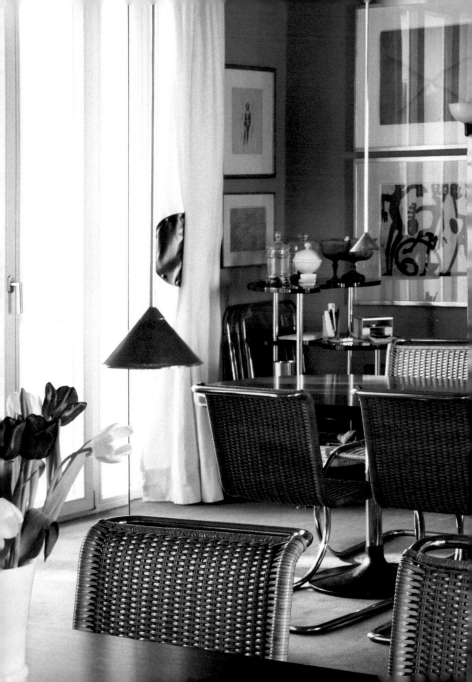

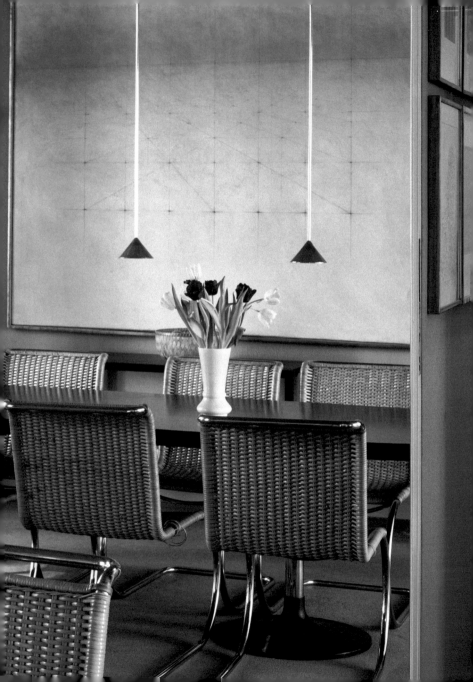

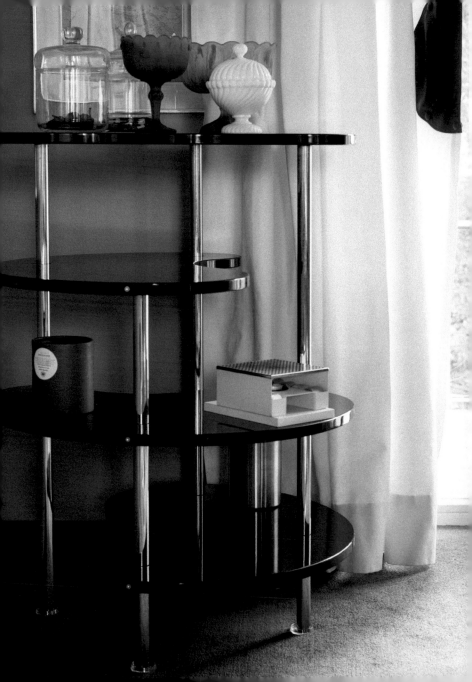

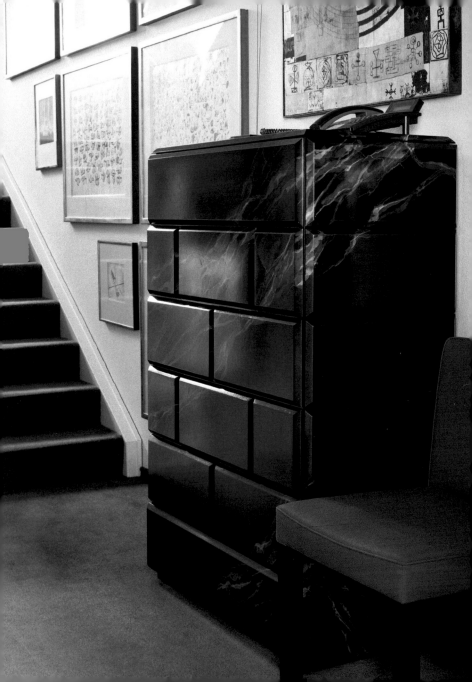

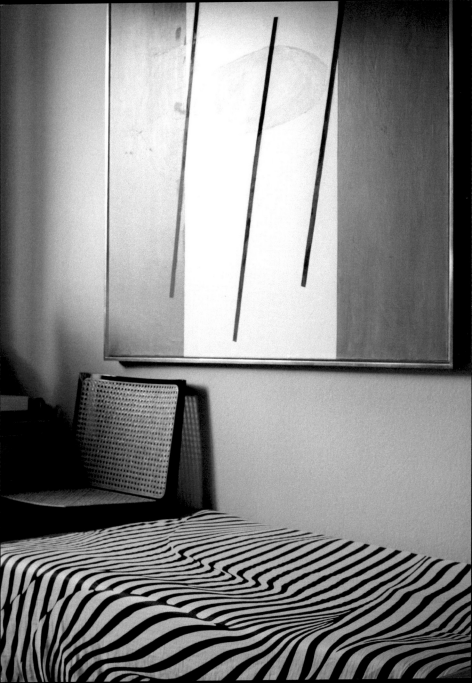

FRANCE, LUXEMBOURG, BELGIUM

LES PRESSES DU RÉEL, DIJON, FR

LESPRESSESDUREEL.COM


UNITED KINGDOM

ANTENNE BOOKS, LONDON, GB

ANTENNEBOOKS.COM


UNITED STATES

ARTBOOK / D.A.P., NEW YORK, US

ARTBOOK.COM


JAPAN

TWELVEBOOKS, TOKYO, JP

TWELVE-BOOKS.COM


AUSTRALIA, NEW ZEALAND

PERIMETER DISTRIBUTION, MELBOURNE, AU

PERIMETERDISTRIBUTION.COM


OTHER COUNTRIES

EDITION PATRICK FREY, ZÜRICH, CH

EDITIONPATRICKFREY.COM

FIRST EDITION EDITION PATRICK FREY, 2021

PRINT RUN    800 COPIES

ISBN 978-3-907236-38-3


PRINTED IN GERMANY

EDITION PATRICK FREY, LIMMATSTRASSE 268, 8005 ZÜRICH, CH

WWW.EDITIONPATRICKFREY.COM

MAIL@EDITIONPATRICKFREY.CH

DISTRIBUTION


SWITZERLAND

AVA VERLAGSAUSLIEFERUNG, AFFOLTERN AM ALBIS, CH

AVA.CH


GERMANY, AUSTRIA

GVA GEMEINSAME VERLAGSAUSLIEFERUNG, GÖTTINGEN, DE

GVA-VERLAGE.DE

TRIX + ROBERT HAUSSMANN

EIN LEBEN MIT DER KUNST UND KÜNSTLER:INNEN

A LIFE WITH ART AND ARTISTS


TEXT

TRIX + ROBERT HAUSSMANN, DIETER SCHWARZ

EDITOR

MARC JANCOU

EDITING

ANDREAS KOLLER AND TEO SCHIFFERLI

TRANSLATION

CATHERINE SCHELBERT

PROOFREADING

JACOB BLANDY, MIRIAM WIESEL

PHOTO CREDITS

ROB GNANT, DORIS QUARELLA, MATTHIAS BUSER, WULF BRACKROCK,

ALFRED HABLÜTZEL, PETER KOPP, TIMOTHY STANDRING,

RITA PALANIKUMAR, LUKAS WASSMANN

DESIGN

TEO SCHIFFERLI

IMAGE EDITING AND COLOR SEPARATION

PAOLA CAPUTO

PRINTED AND BOUND BY DZA, DRUCKEREI ZU ALTENBURG GMBH

PAPER FOR TEXT

MUNKEN PRINT WHITE 1.8 100 G

PAPER FOR PHOTOGRAPHS

MAXI GLOSS 135 G

COVER

CHROMOLUX MAGIC SILVER 250 G

Philipp Schibig
Carl Schmid
Charlotte Schmid
Robert Schmid
Hugo Schumacher
Johannes Robert
    Schürch
Martin Schwarz
Hans Sigg
Peter Sigrist
Gottlieb Soland
Jesús Rafael Soto
Louis Soutter
Pravoslav Sovak
Daniel Spoerri
Jürg Stäuble
Felix Stöckli
Peter Storrer
Erika Streit
Hugo Suter
Takis
André Thomkins
Manina Tischler
Roland Topor
Max Truninger
Varlin
Bernar Venet
Maja Vieli-Bisig
Carlo Vivarelli

Felix Waske
Ilse Weber
Willy Weber
David Weiss
Stefan Wewerka
Max Wiederkehr
Oscar Wiggli
Hans Witschi
Mireille Wunderly
Marianne Wydler-Hersh
Franz Anatol Wyss
Rudolf Zehnder
Muz Zeier
Andreas Züst
Stefan Zwicky

Hans Jörg Glattfelder
Camille Graeser
Robert Graham
Christoph Gredinger
Pierre Haubensak
Erwin Heerich
Otto Heigold
Max Hellstern
Jeroen Henneman
Josef Herzog
Sibylle Heusser
David Hockney
Alfred Hofkunst
Berndt Höppner
Max Hunziker
Rolf Iseli
Johannes Itten
Emanuel Jacob
Max Jenny
Alfred Jensen
Utz Kampmann
Heiner Kielholz
Friedrich Kuhn
Rolf Lehmann
Kaspar-Thomas Lenk
Sol LeWitt
Richard Paul Lohse
Jenny Losinger-Ferri
Bernhard Luginbühl

Bernhard Lüthi
Klaus Lutz
Juan Martinez
Gregory Masurovsky
Max Matter
Gaspare Otto Melcher
Otto Meyer-Amden
László Moholy-Nagy
Giorgio Morandi
Otto Müller
Werner Jakob Müller
Willy Müller-Brittnau
Georges Noël
Beat Odermatt
Meret Oppenheim
Robin Page
Georg Karl Pfahler
Peter Phillips
Markus Raetz
Urs Raussmüller
Sigismund Righini
Aldo Rossi
Dieter Roth
Christian Rothacher
Nelly Rudin
Alex Sadkowsky
Michel Sauer
Xanti Schawinsky
Paolo Scheggi

## KÜNSTLER:INNEN IN DER SAMMLUNG

## ARTISTS IN THE COLLECTION

Hans Aeschbacher
Volker Albus
Horst Antes
Hans Arp
Christian Ludwig Attersee
Pierre Baltensperger
Carlos Barberá
Suzanne Baumann
Moritz Baumgartl
Raffael Benazzi
Ueli Berger
Miguel Berrocal
Joseph Beuys
Guido Biasi
Jakob Bill
Max Bill
Bram Bogart
Jürgen Brodwolf
Anton Bruhin
Michael Buthe
Antonio Calderara
Gianfredo Camesi
Andreas Christen
Miguel Condé
Klaus Däniker
Lucio Del Pezzo
Trudi Demut
Margaretha Dubach
Markus Dulk
Simone Eberli, Andrea Mantel
Franz Eggenschwiler
Anton Egloff
Heinrich Eichmann
Peter Erni
Roland Faesser
Alekos Fassianos
Franz Fédier
Hans Fischli
Bendicht Fivian
Werner Frei
Hanny Fries
Günter Fruhtrunk
Aldo Galli
Ferdinand Gehr
Rupprecht Geiger
Johannes Geuer
Diego Giacometti
Esther Gisler

BILDNACHWEIS

PHOTO CREDITS

| | |
|---|---|
| Rob Gnant | 1969 |
| Doris Quarella | 1973 |
| Matthias Buser | 1976 |
| Wulf Brackrock | 1979 |
| Alfred Hablützel | 1982 |
| Peter Kopp | 1998 |
| Timothy Standring | 2011 |
| Rita Palanikumar | 2012 |
| Lukas Wassmann | 2013 |
| Lukas Wassmann | 2015 |
| Rita Palanikumar | 2015 |

DS    Another Swiss mannerist who deserves mention is Bernhard Luginbühl, not the young, constructivist and stringent sculptor with his C-elements, but the late Luginbühl with the Atlas spheres and his delight in storytelling. He would fit in this context, and Jean Tinguely, too.

TH    Maybe the difference is how much thought has been invested; for us mannerism is not just a spontaneous gesture.

DS    When I think about "*Manierismo critico*," your work with Studio Alchimia, and your connection with Memphis, you could have turned towards Italian art as well. Quite a lot would actually have been compatible with your affinities, from Giorgio de Chirico onwards. But all I see here is the small painting by Antonio Calderara.

RH    There is also a beautiful work by Aldo Rossi that shows the defining elements of his architecture—the columns, the gable with a circular hole. At the 1980 Architecture Biennale in Venice, he built his "Teatro del mondo" on a ship; it was exceptionally beautiful. He was like the colleagues at Studio Alchimia, who had no idea if what they were producing was art or not.

TH      The last thing we did together was to plan "L'uomo architetto," an exhibition for Alchimia's fortieth anniversary. Alessandro Guerriero, founder of Alchimia, invited all the old comrades. The specifications for the contributions were very strict—the item was not to be taller than 35 centimeters—and there was a deadline. We took that very seriously; we made our object that exact size and sent it in on time, but we were the only ones.

RH      In part, the purchase of artworks was by chance; it just happened. Our buying was very unsystematic.

TH      We never believed in a collection strategy.

RH      It was about contrast. As architects we are rational people and that's a good thing. Some of the artists that we knew were outsiders, but outsider architects—that's more unusual.

have in Ibrig, he saw goats grazing and decided to paint a picture with them. He took a sheet of paper, covered it with paint and then with salt. The goats came and licked the salt off—they got colored tongues—and that's how the picture was painted. When Johannes lived with us, he often stayed up late, drawing and drinking, in the morning I would find a sheet of paper on which he had written some advice for the following day, like once, for example, "Dear Trix, today nix."

RH     Anton Bruhin was a good friend, too. I really liked his diversity: he played the mouth harp, painted figurative pictures, did calligraphy, and was a writer. His heroic songs, written in an invented medieval language, were particularly interesting. In 2006 he had an exhibition at Silvia Steiner's gallery in Biel titled "Schöne Bilder" ("Beautiful Pictures")!

DS     He wrote palindromes and those are mirrors too, linguistic mirrors.

RH     I particularly like the picture of the Bauhaus member Xanti Schawinsky. He used a technique for it that he invented himself. He would wrinkle up the canvas and then apply paint with a spray gun to get random effects. I also want to mention Hans Witschi. I think he's a very good painter.

ly shows his interest in language but it is also a record of the days when he used to meet artists like Thomkins and Daniel Spoerri. They were constantly playing with words and coming up with puns. We have one of Spoerri's *Fallenbilder* ("Snare Pictures"). It was badly hung and once fell off the wall, so we glued it back together somehow, but the main thing we asked ourselves was what to do with a fallen *Fallenbild*? Thomkins was often our guest in Zurich and would spend some time with us when we needed a little detachment from his family in Essen.

DS    It was through Thomkins that you met Johannes Geuer from Düsseldorf, wasn't it?

TH    Yes, and then through Geuer's exhibition at Galerie Stähli, Langenbacher + Wankmiller in Lucerne. But Geuer soon fell out with the gallery as he later also did with many others.

RH    What fascinates me about Geuer is his painterly skill, combined with his ideas, for instance, in his painting after Picasso's *Villa Californie* or in the classical interior with snow-covered furniture …

TH    … or the interior under water that he installed in an aquarium. He was bursting with ideas and constantly inventing things. Once when he was spending a few weeks in the old farmhouse that we

RH        … in reduced and constructed form, initially as models. We realized that so-called postmodernism required a clear concept and so I tried to formulate it in words.

DS        Looking around your home, one gets the impression that many of the drawings and pictures that you have hung up feature aspects of "*Manierismo critico.*" André Thomkins is probably the most stringent representative of critical mannerism in your collection.

RH        Thomkins was a very good friend of ours. We met him in 1969 when he exhibited with Felix Handschin in Basel, or probably even earlier through Paul Gredinger and Markus Kutter of the GGK advertising agency, for which we had done various jobs. I was particularly taken with his palindromes and anagrams, his playful use of language.

DS        You contributed a similar invention to the Marconi catalogue—a kind of portmanteau device that made it possible to combine two random terms into a new unit.

TH        I collected Robert's wordplay and published a little book for his seventy-fifth birthday titled *Verlorene Eier – ein gefundenes Fressen* (literally: "Lost [Poached] Eggs—a Found Feast"). It certain-

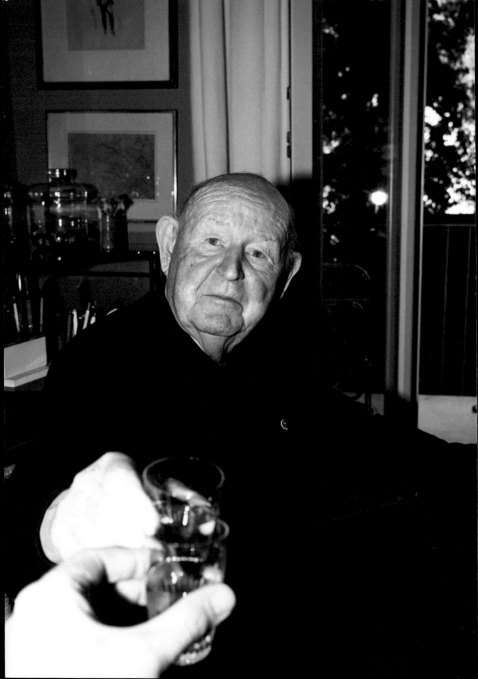

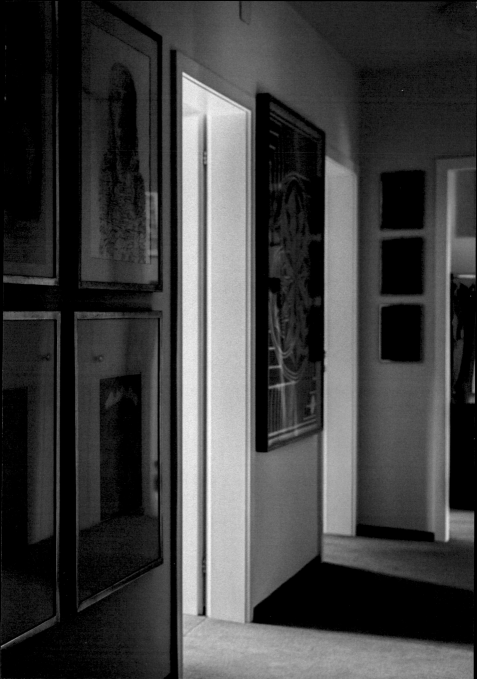

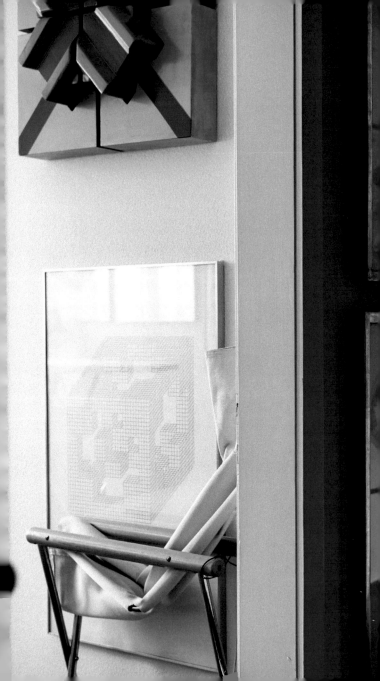

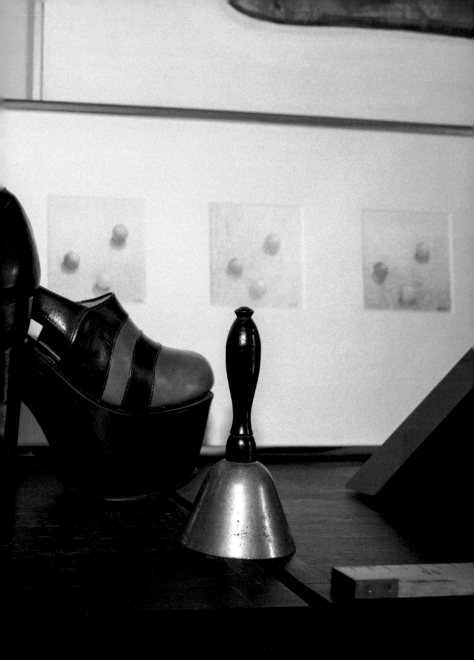

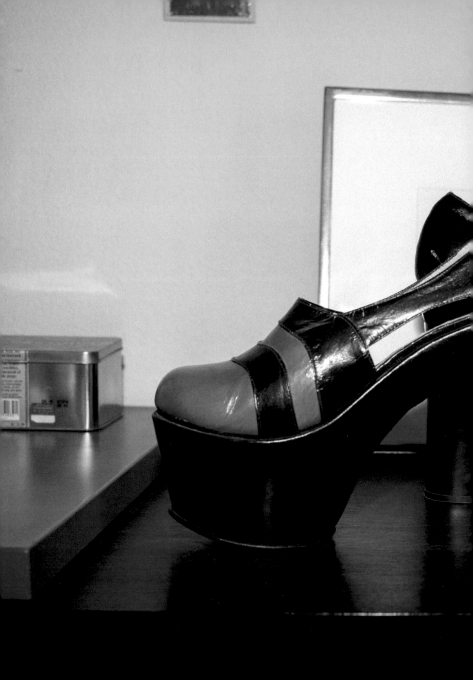

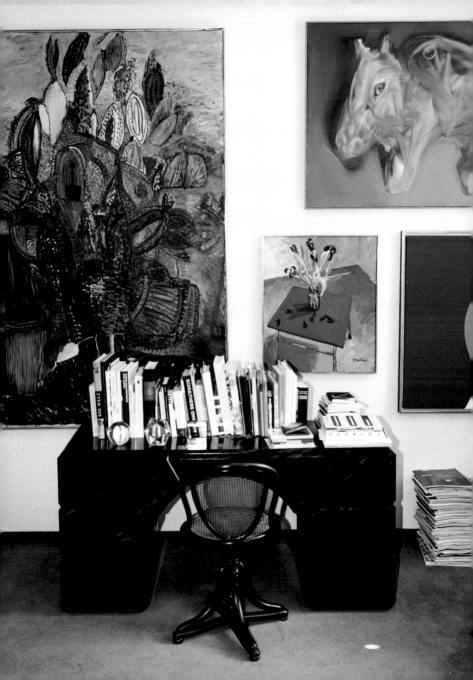

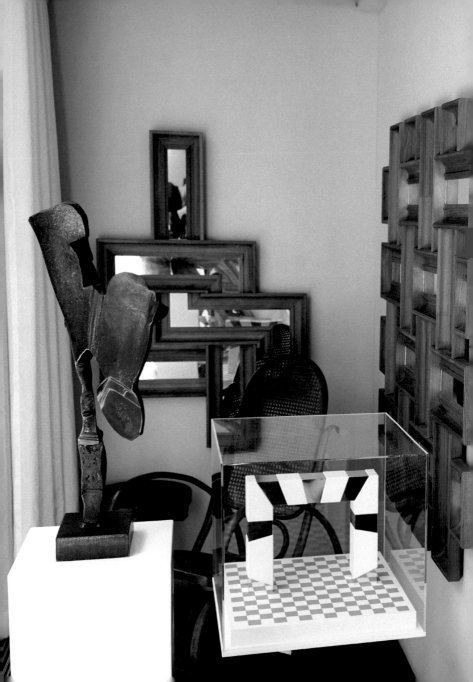

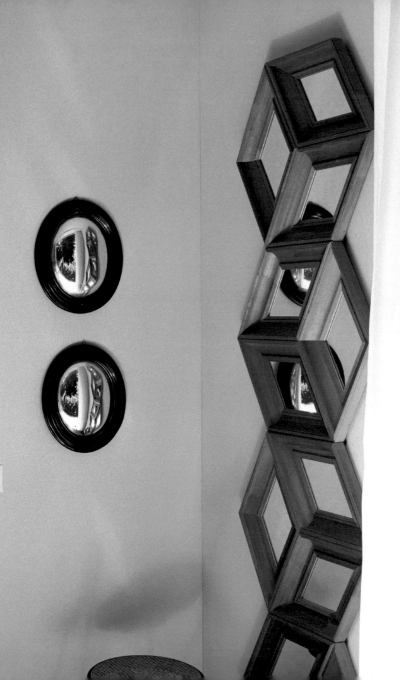

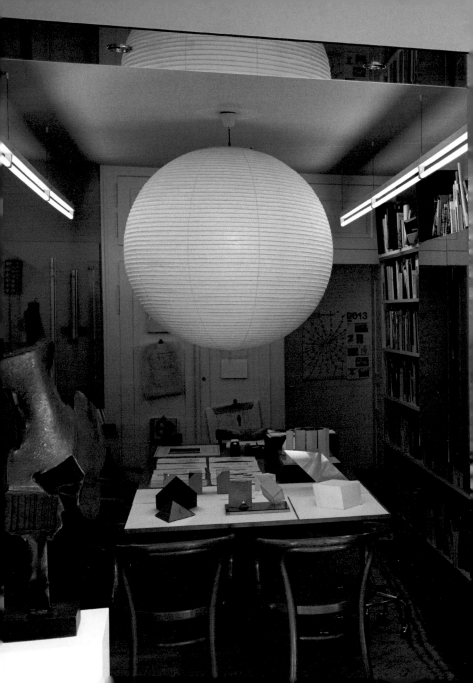

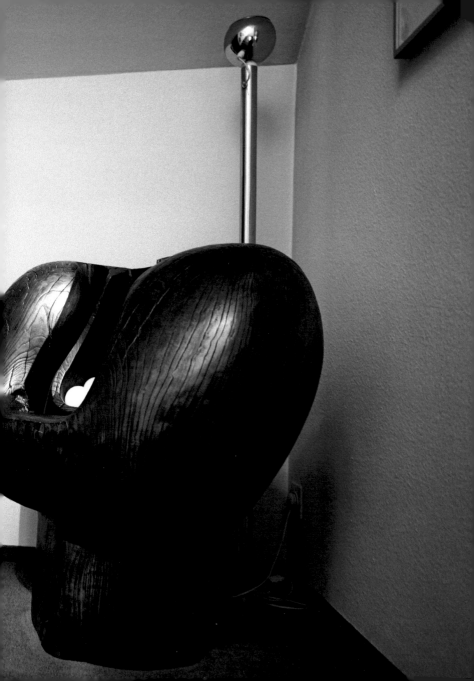

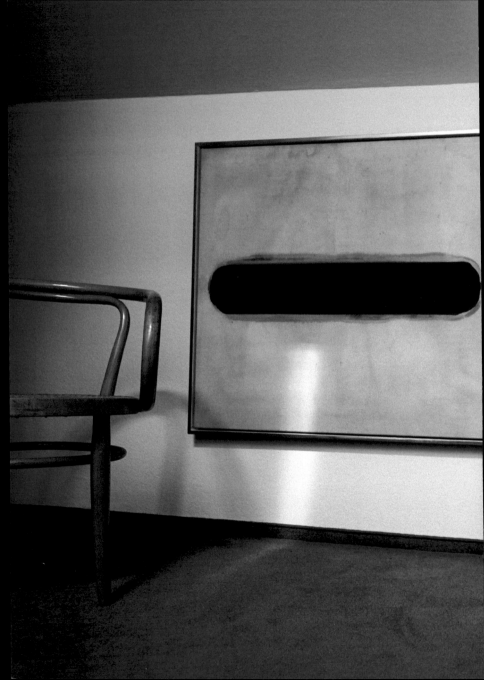

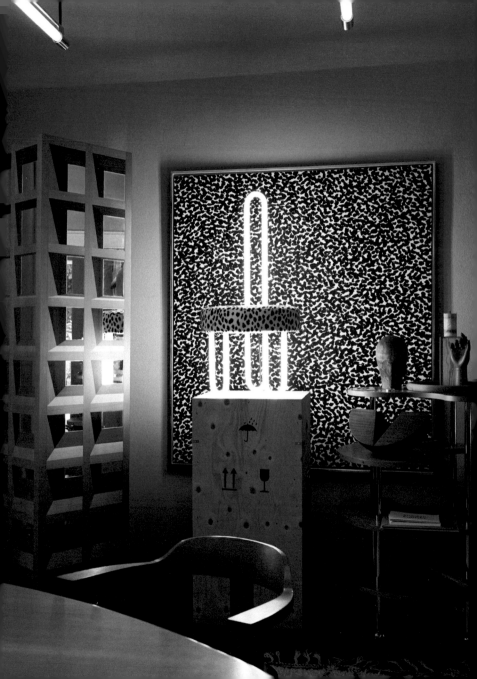

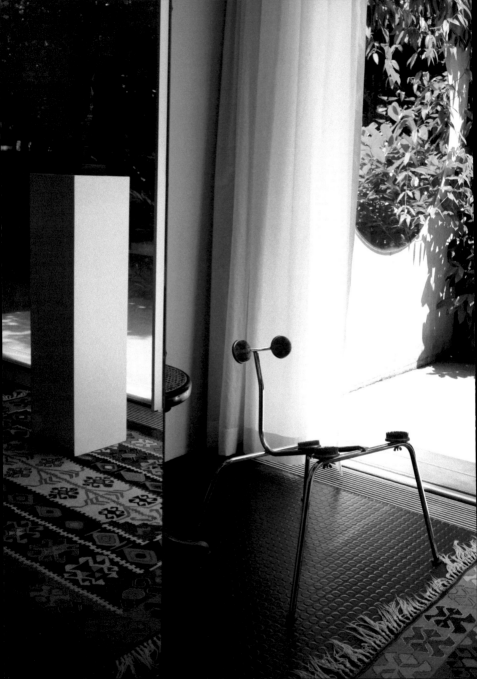

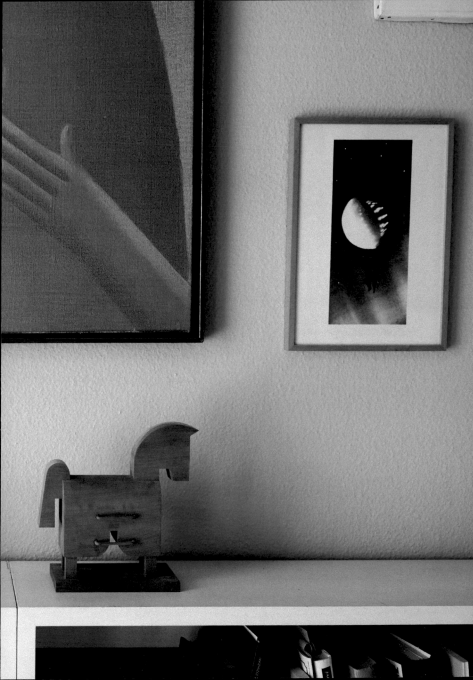

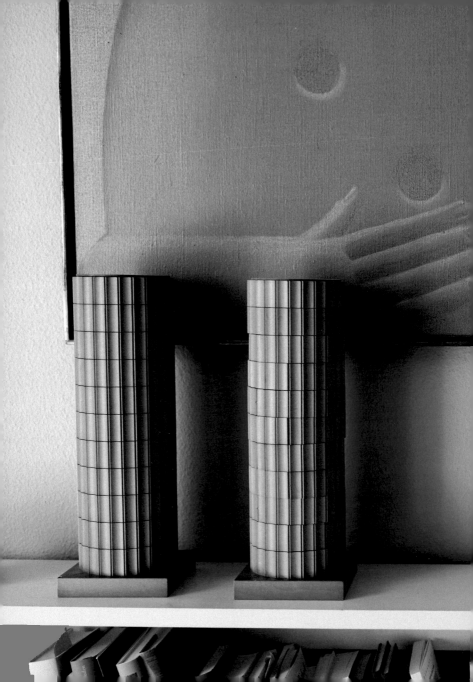

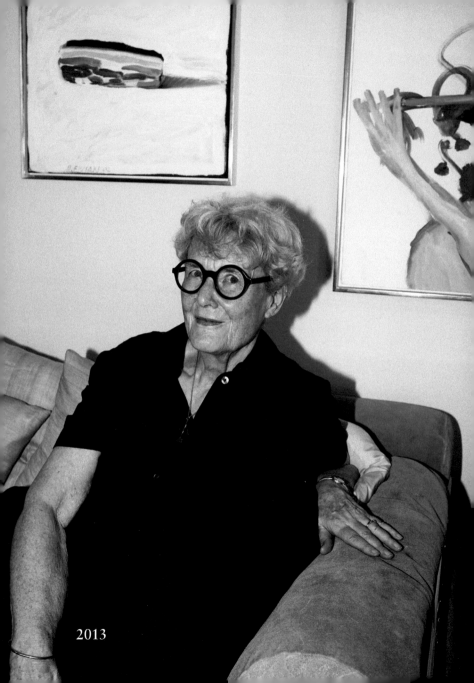

2013

sculpture *Enigma* for the Sculpture Garden Biennial in Geneva.

DS        I would like to ask about "*Manierismo critico*," as you call it. In connection with your work for Studio Marconi in Milan, you wrote an essay for the magazine *Werk, Bauen + Wohnen* (no. 10, 1981), where you spoke about your "search for other means of expression" and a "growing doubt about many dogmas of modernism." You drafted a wide-ranging program that embraced aspects of design such as alienating materials, creating illusionary space through the use of mirrors, illusionist modification of body and space, the use of literary forms, ambivalence, and the involvement of contradiction, disruption, and destruction.

        Did these considerations underpin your approach to art? Did they define your understanding of art?

TH        Classical modernism was an important influence; it was where our teachers came from and then we studied the historical phenomenon of mannerism, because we had the impression that, in many respects, there was something like a mannerist break in the 1980s. It wasn't our thing to throw cobblestones; the break for us was more in the realm of art. And it was important for us to describe these phenomena as object lessons ...

didn't mean so much to me. He rarely exhibited his work, he was an outsider. He worked for me for a while, showing up when he felt like it and then disappearing again. His work is pretty heterogeneous. There are drawings with pop figures and then paintings of mandalas and geometric elements; his late work deals with numerical systems. I took Wiederkehr under my wing and succeeded in getting him a commission to do a relief for the theater restaurant in Ingolstadt.

TH     In 1968, we entered the competition for the Swiss pavilion at Expo '70 in Osaka in collaboration with Markus Raetz. I had met Markus when I was living in Bern and had swapped a small sculpture of mine for a relief of his. Then we bought the relief *Goppenstein*, the pink train window with the little clouds floating next to it on the wall. That's what inspired us to suggest that Markus design a little cloud suitcase for the competition.

RH     He drew up a detailed plan of the suitcase with all of its features, but unfortunately we didn't place in the competition.

TH     Recently we worked with Daniel Sommer, who designs exhibitions at the gta Institute of the ETH and also makes prints of his own. In 2020 he contributed to the development of our large mirror

<sup>DS</sup> Were there any other projects with artists?

<sup>RH</sup> When Heinrich Eichmann was commissioned to create a large wall painting for the new Stadttheater Ingolstadt in 1965, he brought me on board for the interior decoration and recommended me for the lighting. Eichmann was a house painter by profession. In the 1930s, he fought in the Spanish Civil War and was later politically active as the head of the plasterers' and house painters' cooperative in Zurich. He was connected with Zurich's concrete artists after the war and when he retired, he started making art again, ornamental paintings with gold leaf. It was a very special technique. He also used gold leaf when he painted his large mural on the raw concrete wall in Ingolstadt, which was totally unprecedented.

<sup>TH</sup> When we designed the indoor swimming pool of the Mont Cervin Hotel in Zermatt in 1970, we commissioned Eichmann to do the mural. Afterwards, the client tried to bring down the price but Eichmann said, "Do you know what, as an artist, I am closer to God than you are."

<sup>RH</sup> I met the artist Max Wiederkehr at the School of Arts and Crafts where he was a draftsman. I bought numerous drawings from him when he needed money. Wiederkehr lived in Zurich, went to India in the 1960s and lived in an esoteric world that

Then I had an accident: I went to light a cigarette and the matchbook caught fire in my right hand. I was pretty badly burnt. Diego came running, accompanied us out and took us to his workshop. He bandaged my hand with great expertise and we were deeply impressed by how well he did it. We met several times at the Café Les Deux Magots in Paris. Then we would decide to have dinner at Lipp but it was booked up every time so we had to go some-place else—it was always the same ritual.

DS     But the brothers are not represented in your collection?

TH     Yes, we have two alabaster lamps by Diego. We would have liked to have a table, too, and Diego made a note of our order but every time we came to Paris, somebody had already been there ahead of us and had purchased the table. The great collectors of Zurich high society were served first …

RH     It was too late for a work by Alberto. For a while we had a seated figure in bronze for review at home from Gimpel & Hanover but it was already too expensive for us.

TH     Many times we would have liked to have work by someone that we knew well but it somehow never happened.

DS        Did Diego take the lead on this project? He also did the casts in bronze for Alberto.

RH        Yes, he was entirely responsible for carrying out the project.

DS        It seems surprising that in this phase of his life, when he was making the portrait busts of Eli Lotar, Alberto chose to work on a decorative project again.

RH        That's because of his friendship with Zumsteg—an incredible stroke of luck. Alberto had a small studio with an attic and Diego had his workshop next door, like a blacksmith's shop. Alberto worked with plaster on armatures Diego had prepared for him. Diego sensed what Alberto needed; he was clearly the helper. The two brothers had their own completely distinctive way of speaking to each other; it was a symbiosis.

DS        Were you still in touch with Diego after Alberto died?

RH        Yes. Diego even rescued me once! Zumsteg had invited us to a Parisian fashion show with a *grand dîner* and I felt extremely out of place. Diego was there too and I could tell from far away that he felt just as uncomfortable as I did.

He asked me if I would take on the job and I immediately had ideas about how a beautiful bar could look. The next time we met, we had both taken along publications on the Kärntner Bar in Vienna that Adolf Loos designed—it's rare that a client and architect have the same vision of a project.

TH      You spoke about the lighting and said you had always drafted the lamps yourself but that you had somebody else in mind this time, who was especially good at it.

RH      I told Zumsteg how much I liked the lamps Alberto and Diego Giacometti made in the 1930s, when they were designing decorative items for the Parisian furniture designer Jean-Michel Frank. I had never actually seen them, only pictures in books. Zumsteg told me they were both friends of his and asked if I had time to drive to Paris with him the following Wednesday. We met Diego there and I basically worked only with him. Alberto I met only once, when both brothers came to Zurich to show me the lamps. I had prepared a plywood model so that you could see how high the bar was, and there was also a prototype of the chairs. The plaster model that they brought along had cheap glass balls. I suggested alabaster because the effect of this material combined with bronze is very beautiful, and they were delighted.

DS      Was it perhaps related to the fact that Jensen was not a constructivist like Zurich's concrete artists, but rather had something that might be identified as mannerist through the synthesis of the numerical systems of the Maya with those of Greek antiquity?

TH      There was something esoteric about Jensen with his numerical mysticism that fascinated us.

RH      It was as if he had a religion of his own; the work radiated great strength. And Jensen's work with grids inspired me to explore the potential of graph paper — you can do so much with it, practically anything from trompe-l'oeil to construction.

DS      The design of the Kronenhalle-Bar in 1965 gave you the chance to collaborate with Alberto and Diego Giacometti.

RH      It started with Gustav Zumsteg approaching me and asking if I had time to discuss something with him. He was very mysterious; he didn't want his mother Hulda Zumsteg, who ran the Kronenhalle, to know about it. It was a Sunday afternoon when we met and he told me that he wanted to open a bar in the hair salon next to the Kronenhalle. This salon was made out of mahogany by the way…

wasn't sandstone but just metal cladding. The gallery was on the ground floor and we created a new room below street level so that you could make a circular tour, walking down a set of stairs when you entered the gallery into an elongated room, and then climbing up into a smaller room at the rear and back to the entrance from the inner courtyard.

DS      The variations in the spatial situation allowed for ever new surprises in the dramaturgy of hanging the exhibitions. The narrow rooms on two levels had a singular charm, especially against the backdrop of the tall walls around the inner courtyard where sculptures were exhibited.

But back to your collection. The German painters Horst Antes, Geiger and Pfahler, the Belgian Bram Bogart and the American Alfred Jensen are international artists, who stand out because your collection consists mainly of art from Switzerland. They didn't belong to your circle of friends but they were represented by Swiss galleries like Ziegler and also Kornfeld in Bern.

RH      Jensen was an extraordinary figure, different from anything we had ever experienced.

TH      I learned about Jensen in Bern, because Adolf Max Vogt's brother Werner had bought three large paintings at Kornfeld that impressed me.

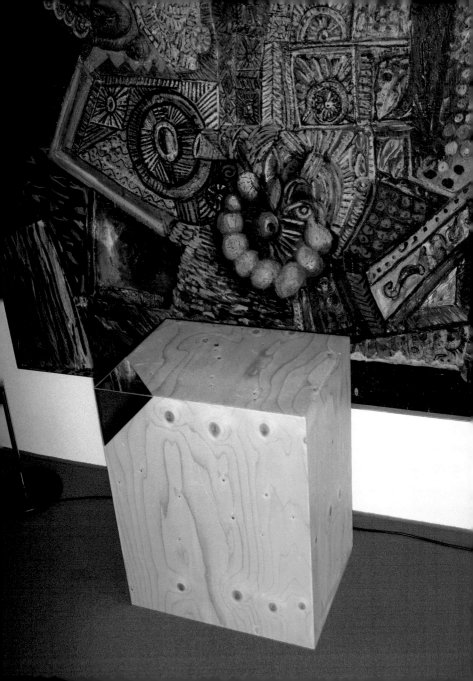

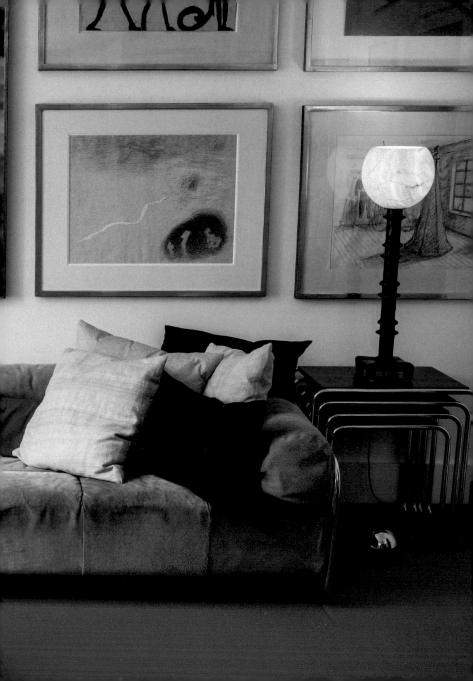

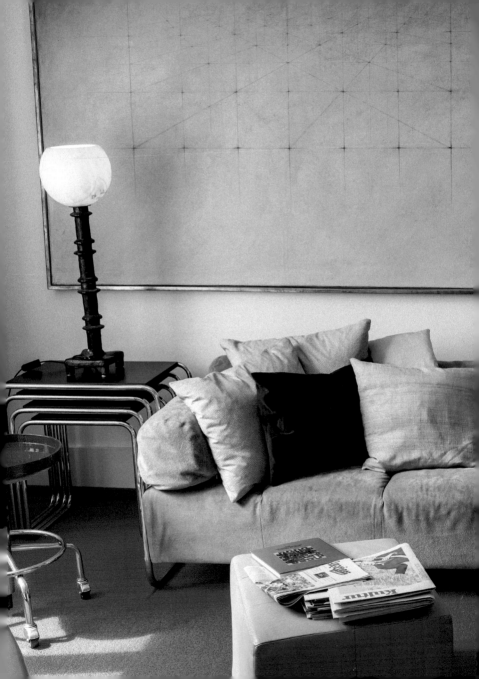

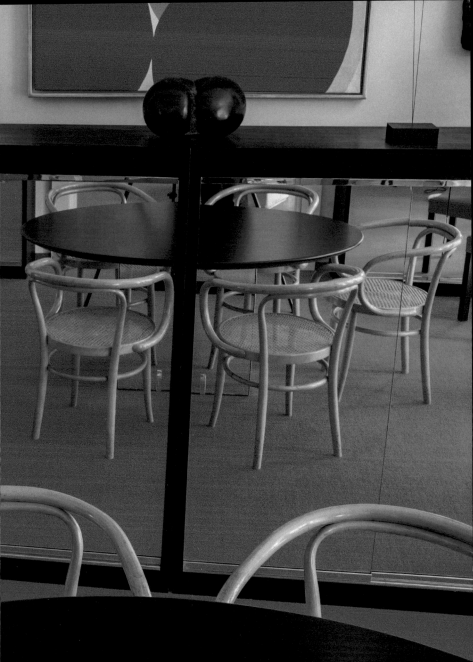

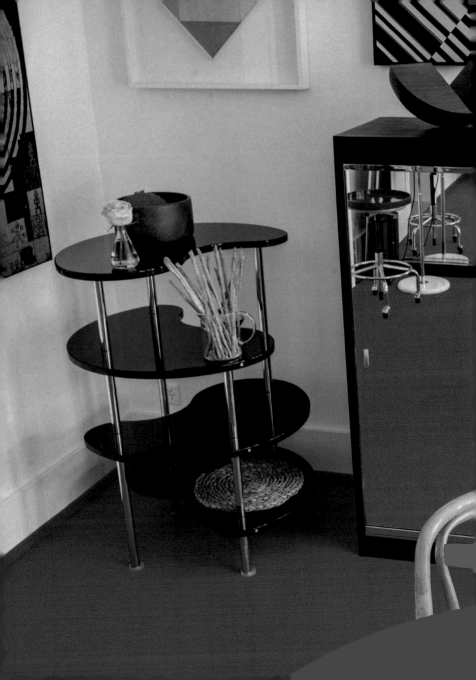

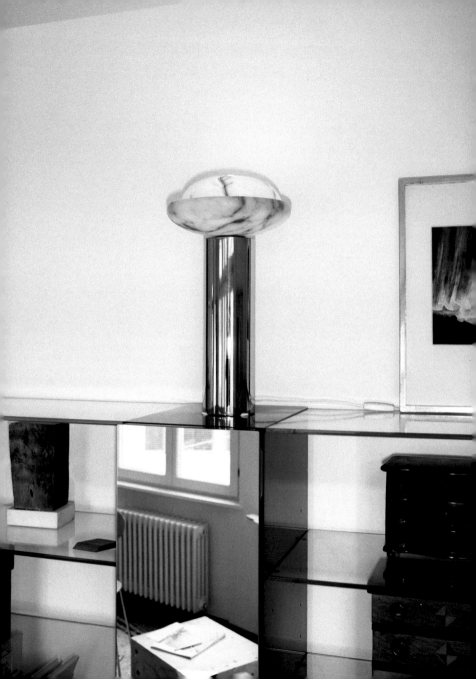

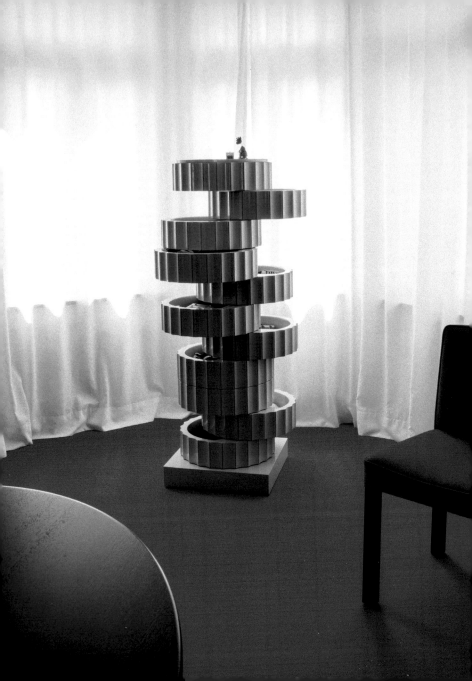

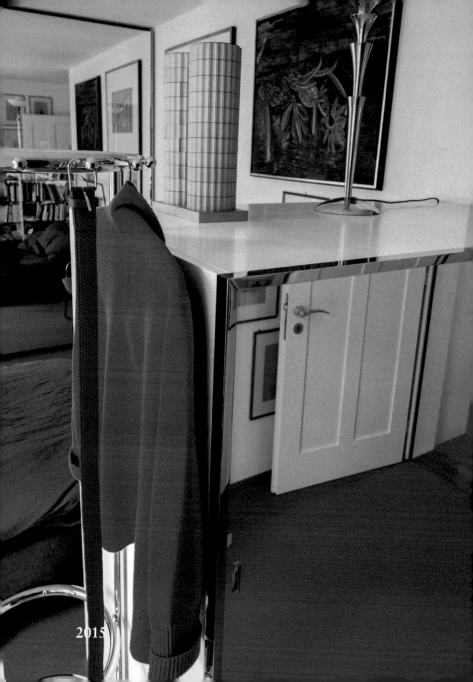

2015

when the Gimpel & Hanover Gallery moved into their new premises on Claridenstrasse in Zurich in 1962. It was not actually a project; I just made suggestions about how to make better use of the space. I thought about how to deal with what was once a store with a big window and no storage space. I developed movable room-height walls placed in front of the actual walls so that you could hang pictures invisibly behind them. In front there were exhibition walls that simultaneously concealed the real walls. Sometimes I contributed to the design of the exhibitions, too, but not with architectural measures.

DS      An important project was the design of the Maeght Gallery in Zurich in 1968.

RH      Contact with Aimé and Marguerite Maeght in Paris came about through the silk merchant and art collector Gustav Zumsteg. I was first commissioned in 1967 to renovate the Maeght Gallery on Rue de Téhéran in Paris. The metal cladding of the gallery façade and the base of the building never came about. I don't really know why the project petered out. The Zurich project started because my brother bought the building on Predigerplatz that had to be completely renovated and refurbished. We worked with the historic preservation office and designed sandstone frames for the windows but it turned out that the supposedly historical façade

I was able to arrange a commission for Otto, in 1979 for example at the old botanical garden in Zurich, where we converted the existing buildings into a Museum of Ethnography with the architects Hans and Annemarie Hubacher, and in 2001 for the court-yard of the office building in Heiligkreuz built by Toni Bargetze in Vaduz, where we designed the interior. I once took Otto and Trudi along on a trip to France. It was a wonderful experience to discover and study buildings with them. Trudi kept a record of everything in her diary. That was the first time that I saw Le Corbusier's Notre-Dame du Haut in Ronchamp.

The artists we met with were all so different, so distinct. We would talk about what was happening in the art world, and also argue. Otto Müller, Hans Aeschbacher, Heinrich Eichmann, and Hans Fischli all did sculpture—friends, enemies, estranged...

DS     As of the 1960s, there were several galleries in Zurich that made an important contribution to introducing new, international art.

RH     We regularly visited galleries in Zurich: Bruno Bischofberger, Renée und Maurice Ziegler, Gimpel & Hanover, and Pierre Baltensperger. Since Willy Rotzler's wife Anne and Erika Brausen were friends of mine in London, I was actively involved

RH     The studios that Ernst Gisel designed at Wuhrstrasse in Zurich in 1953 were extraordinary. Gisel and the painter Max Truninger really made a great effort to have those studios built for artists. They applied to companies for financing and were successful. Friedrich Kuhn had a studio there and so did Muz Zeier, Trudi Demut, and Otto Müller.

TH     Otto Müller and Trudi Demut were close friends of ours. Apart from her sculptures, Trudi Demut had the ability to make anything look beautiful, even her modest apartment. She gave us bronze maquettes of her important works; they are often very delicate and show most clearly how sensitive she was. We acquired a large plaster piece of hers and two paintings.

RH     What impressed me about Otto Müller was the way he would simplify the shape of an object. You can see this especially well in his heads; he was obsessed with them.

TH     Like his bronze relief *Frau Welt* ("Mrs. World"), which is not a woman anymore but has become a powerful, expressive figure because he left out all the details.

RH     We acquired sculptures of his and also one large and several small drawings. A couple of times

was too tall and we had no room for it; besides, it was embarrassing to have a picture of myself on the wall behind me.

There was a special circle of people around Varlin on the Rindermarkt in Zurich; it included very different artists like Leo Leuppi, Colette Ryter, who wove carpets after designs by Jean Lurçat, and Henry Wabel. They would get together late mornings for a drink at the Klosterbräu and sometimes they'd keep going until midnight.

DS    And the circle around Friedrich Kuhn?

RH    I bought my first picture by Kuhn at the Christmas exhibition in the Helmhaus. After that, he would always come to me when he was broke. I would give him some money and tell him he should give me something for it, so I ended up with a lot of paintings by him.

TH    I had hardly met any bohemian artists like that before. I appreciated the work of Friedrich Kuhn, but was a little put off because he was so unrestrained. Dieter Roth was like that too. He was always doing something unexpected. But we have wonderful memories of Hanny Fries; she was a good friend of ours.

When my father died in 1955, I set up business with my brother on Oberdorfstrasse because I wanted to get away from period furniture and wallpaper. There were rooms in the back where I had my drafting table to work on interior architecture. My furniture was sold in the store but there wasn't much at first. We established a lot of contacts that way. I particularly remember Varlin. I only have one painting by him although he was a close friend. Varlin wanted to paint a double portrait of me and my brother because we both had red hair. Around the same time, he finished a portrait of his future wife Franca wearing an ocelot coat. The pattern of the fur dominated the whole picture and Varlin had the idea that he could do something similar with our hair. I offered to buy fabric of the same color for him as a backdrop. Varlin thought that when you do a double portrait, one of the sitters loses out. So I said, "Willy, why not make two canvases and then you can put them side by side afterwards." He agreed, so I went to Racher, the art supply store, to buy frames and marched back with them to the studio on Neumarkt. First he had one of us sit for him, and then the other. Varlin would call when he needed one of us again. That's when I realized that posing is just as strenuous as the work of painting. If I wore a different coat, I got scolded because then he had to repaint the entire picture. I don't have the double portrait because, for one thing, the format

bookstores. Actually, writers were not well represented in the club.

DS      And you Trix?

TH      One by Rupprecht Geiger. I wanted to buy it from Toni Gerber in Bern but then he gave it to me. I really liked Geiger's radiant colors. Years later we also bought some of his prints. Robert bought a picture by Georg Karl Pfahler, when he was at the State Academy of Fine Arts in Stuttgart. He started teaching there in 1986. I was close friends with Gerber while I was still studying. He first exhibited art in his apartment in Bern, and then in his gallery, and that's where I met artists from Bern. Gerber showed the sculptures I had made at the time under the influence of Linck's mobiles. For a while I even thought of going into art and I went to a blacksmith to forge my own works in metal. When I finished my studies at the ETH in 1964, I applied for a federal art grant. Max Bill was one of the jurors and he told me my work was pretty good, but that he had seen my graduate thesis for the ETH and in his opinion I was more talented in that field. That was when I had the opportunity to put up a large spiral in Ernst Gisel's building at Expo 64 in Lausanne.

<sup>DS</sup>    The Giedion circle was followed by the Club Bel Etage, founded in 1954. They met at the Schifflände for a short while and then above the Weisse Kreuz restaurant on Falkenstrasse.

<sup>RH</sup>    I was a founding member of the Club Bel Etage, because I liked the idea of presenting exhibitions in an apartment without it being a gallery. That's where I met Meret Oppenheim, who had just started making art again. Later I bought a drawing from her. The club was founded and run by Gottfried Honegger, but mainly also by his wife Warja Lavater. Actually, there were no collectors in this club; nobody had the money to buy art. But then again, it was an art salon where people met. Bern had a counterpart to the Bel Etage—the Café Commerce on Gerechtigkeitsgasse. Everybody went there, from the architects of Atelier 5 to Teo Jakob with his furniture store to the artists. I knew the people in this circle through my work as a furniture designer.

<sup>DS</sup>    What was the first painting that you bought, Robert?

<sup>RH</sup>    A small one by Emanuel Jacob. I'd met him at the Club Bel Etage. Restaurant Kronenhalle—it was still very modest—was also important in those days, as well as the artists' costume ball and then the

<sup>DS</sup>    Did Max Bill and Richard Paul Lohse also play a role in the Giedion circle?

<sup>RH</sup>    No. I was never really friends with Bill but I was later with Lohse. Bill's self-promotion as a genius was a bit too much for me, although I deeply admired the unity of design to which he aspired. I heard his lecture in 1953 with the motto *Vom Löffel bis zur Stadt* ("From Spoon to City") at the inauguration of the Hochschule für Gestaltung, the school of design in Ulm, and was impressed that somebody wanted to revive the Bauhaus.

<sup>TH</sup>    Lohse was older than we were, already an established artist, and so there was a certain congenial divide. He didn't always agree with what we did, but basically, he appreciated Robert. They had argumentative but friendly conversations. When we went to the first Architecture Biennale in Venice with him in 1980, he told us he would have to break off his friendship with Robert. He thought this time our ideas for the textile designs I was talking about before had really gone too far. Naturally the bit about the friendship was not quite serious, but what he said about the fabrics certainly was.

<sup>RH</sup>    And there was Camille Graeser, who appealed to me, the most sensitive, intelligent, not loud, and not overly ambitious, but a person with substance.

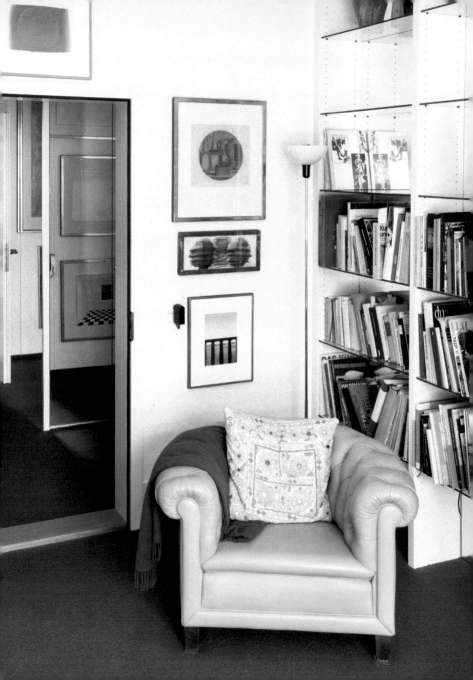

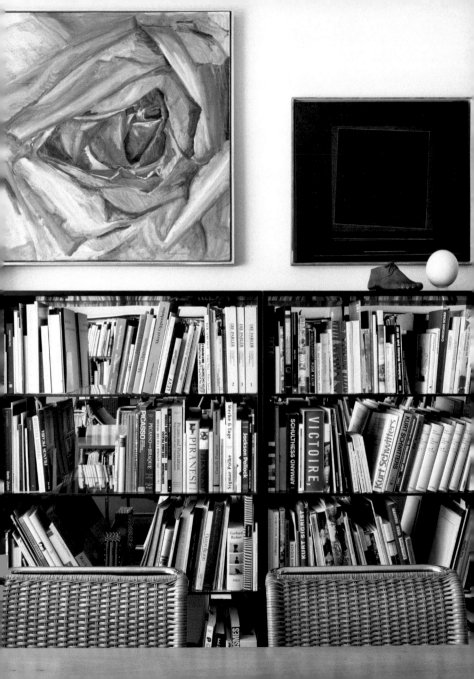

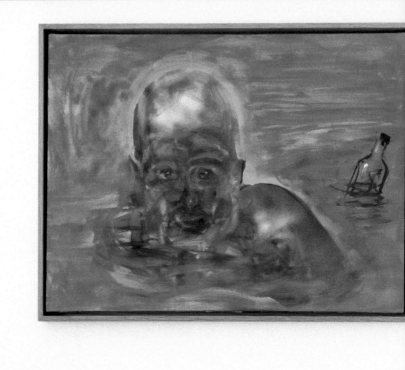
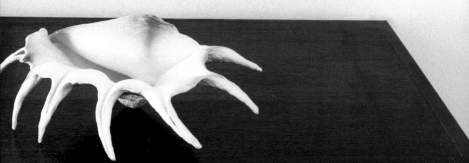

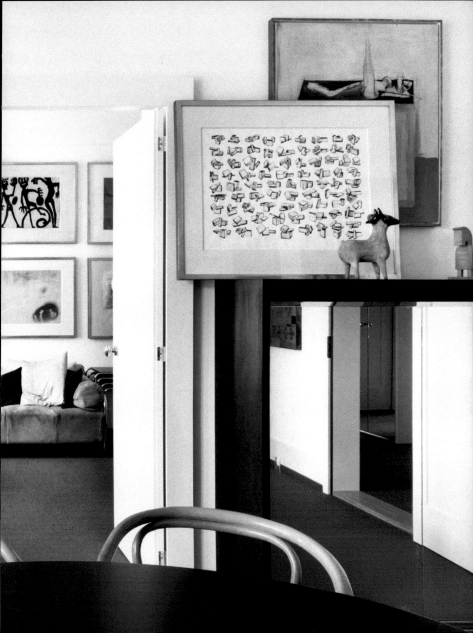

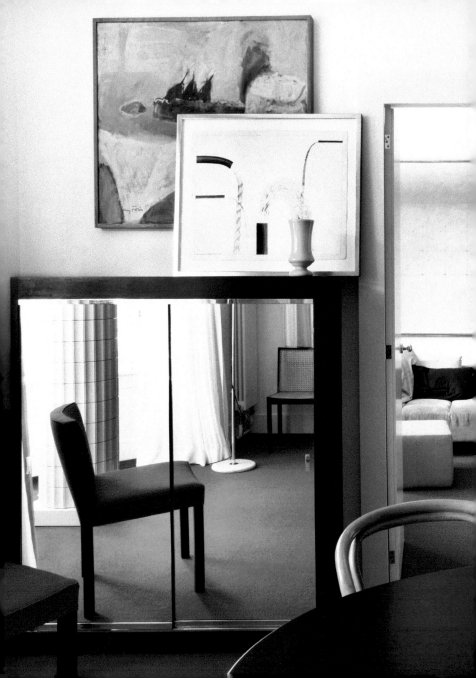

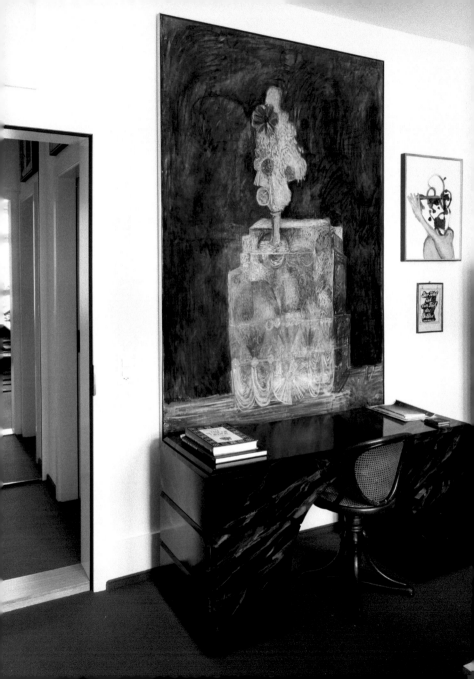

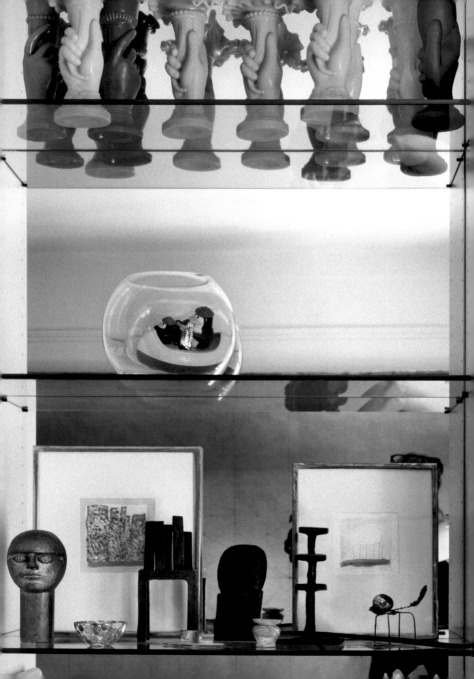

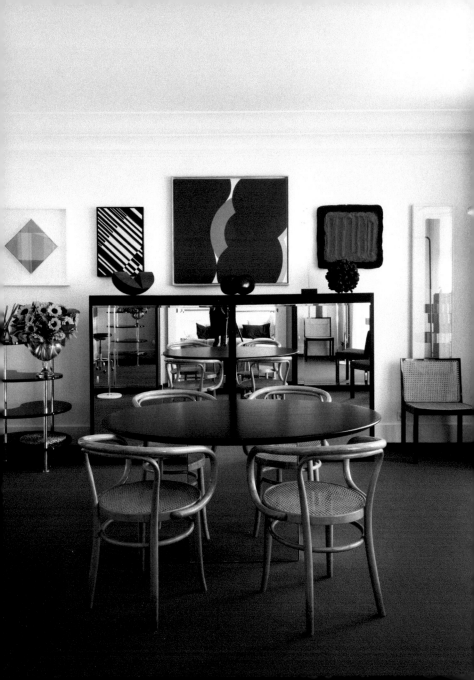

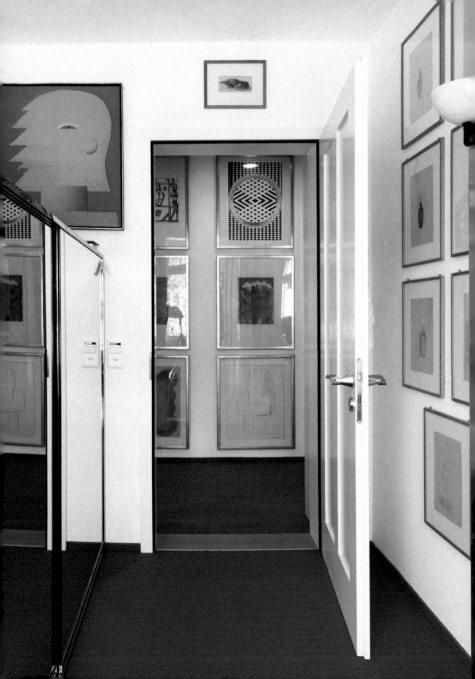

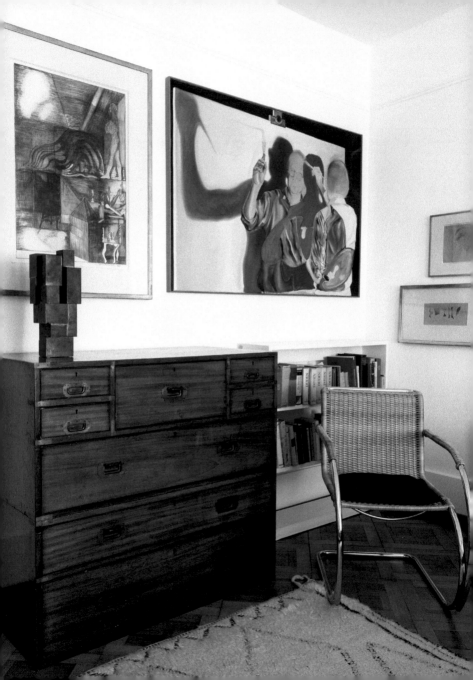

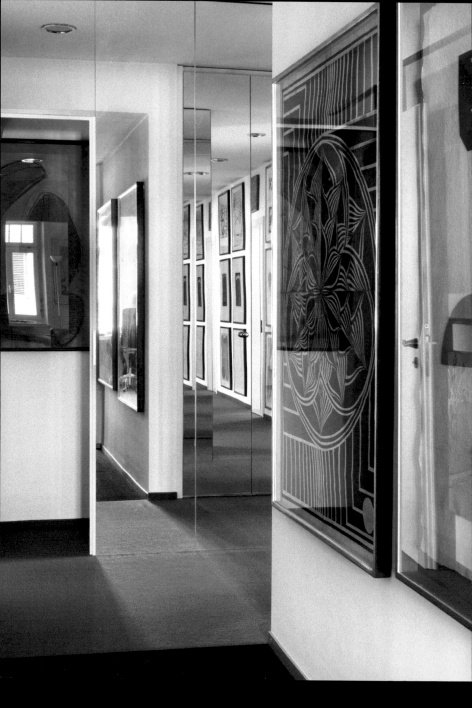

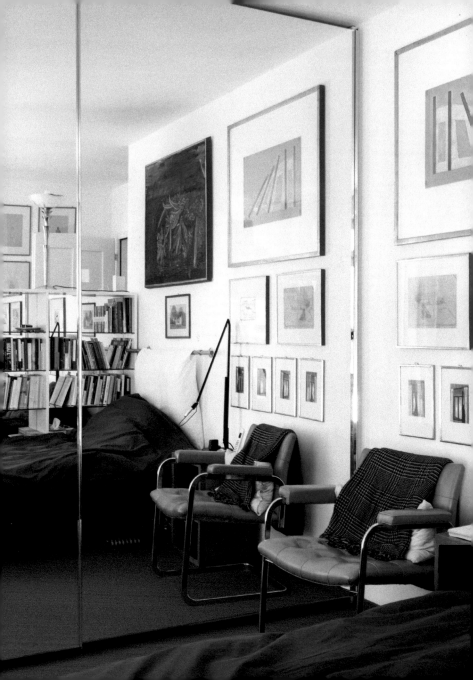

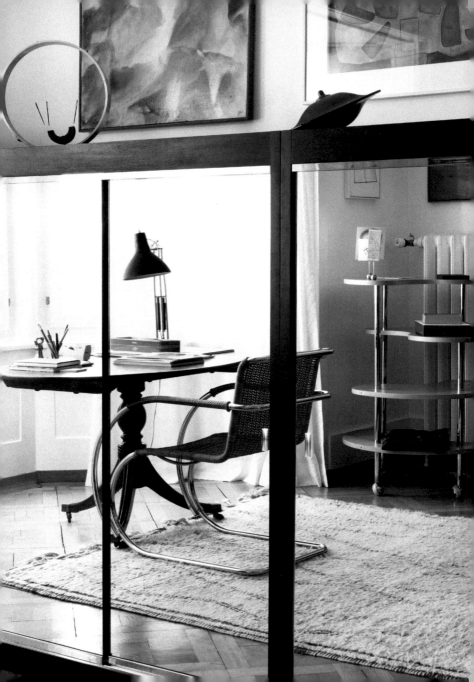

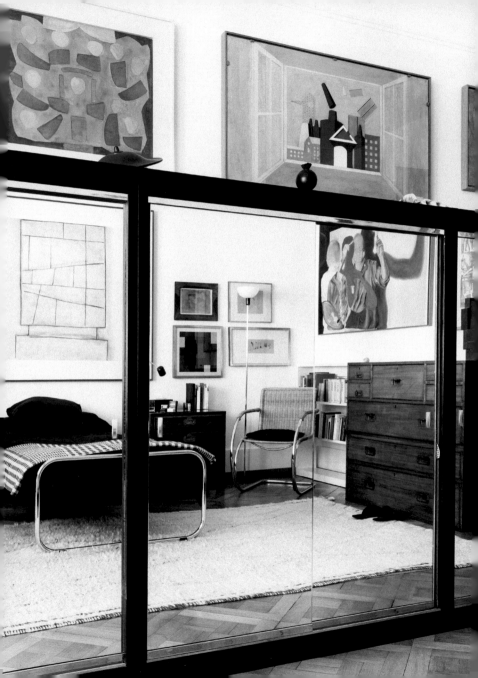

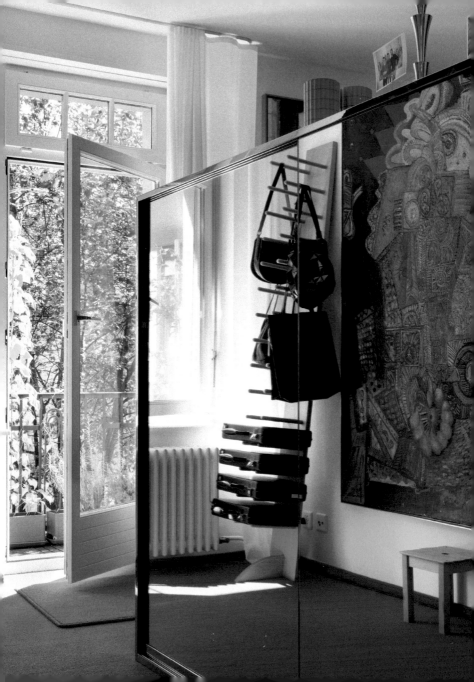

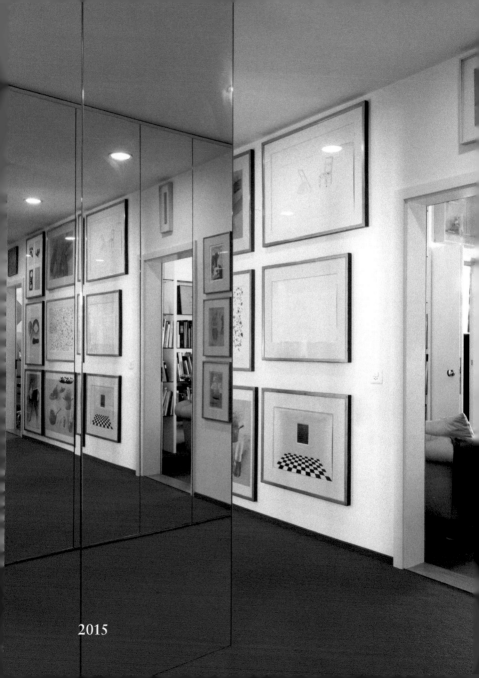

2015

RH     After meeting in Lausanne at Expo 64, we saw each other again in 1966 at a Luginbühl exhibition at Galerie Ziegler in Zurich. We got married in 1967 and founded a design office together. We realized that we had shared interests, in Italian mannerism for instance.

DS     But those were opposing fields—on one hand, constructivism in connection with De Stijl and Walter Linck and on the other hand, mannerism. How did you reconcile them?

TH     We did work with trompe-l'oeil effects, mirrors, virtual spaces, but it was always based on a firm foundation.

DS     And how did the shift from the Giedion circle to mannerism come about?

RH     In the attic at home I found some Czech avant-garde magazines from the 1920s and discovered a picture by Friedrich Vordemberge-Gildewart. He had broken up his constructivist compositions, applying wood, metal, and glass elements. When I was studying in Amsterdam, I visited him and showed him the reproduction. To me the sculptural elements in the pictures were not mannerist but rather an extension of Bauhaus modernism.

("Olympian Spring") bothered him so he painted that white too.

RH    So you were already interested in trompe-l'oeil back then. That really came out in our fabric collection of 1981 for the Mira-X textile company. We transferred basic architectural patterns of fake marble or fake wood to textiles—maybe our most important work of all.

TH    But I started out by studying architecture at the ETH in Zurich. Then I got married, had two children, and moved with my first husband to the United States and then to Mexico. Art didn't play an important role in those days except in Mexico where I came across the work of the architect Luis Barragán at the Casa Pedregal with its strong colors. When I came back, I took up architecture again and finished my studies. An important impetus was Adolf Max Vogt's course on mannerism. I discovered a completely different approach to art.

DS    And how did the two of you meet?

TH    At Expo 64 in Lausanne. I had just graduated and was working as an architect for the office of Gisel Howald Schnebli on the project of the Centre de l'Hôtellerie. Robert was doing the restaurant and designed a chair.

I grew up in Bern in what you might call Bauhaus surroundings. We had Breuer chairs and a lot of my parents' friends were artists. At Christmas, my father used to take us to the so-called Kramgasse exhibition, where all the stores displayed pictures in their windows. In high school I was very good at drawing. When I was about fifteen, I met Walter and Margrit Linck through my parents and they let me paint ceramics in their studio. Actually, only men were allowed to make pottery and the women painted the ceramics. I was deeply impressed by Walter Linck's work and his personality and, at first, I didn't even notice that Margrit Linck also worked as an artist.

I was impressed because the Lincks didn't own a single ugly object—the rooms were just plain beautiful. There was a grapevine growing outside on the wall of the studio and Linck thought it should have grapes, regardless of whether it produced any or not, so he bought artificial grapes and attached them to the vine. I realized that you could do something that's beautiful even if you don't go by the rules.

Later, when I was working for the architect Rudolf Olgiati, I rediscovered this idea of beauty. Optical reality was more important to him than doing justice to materials, which is what I grew up with. He was the antipode of what we learned in our courses at the ETH. Olgiati installed the bookcase in his guest room and painted it white. The purple linen binding of Carl Spitteler's *Olympischer Frühling*

RH      I really admired the collection the Giedions had, the way it was seamlessly integrated into all the books. It was easy to spark my enthusiasm and that rubbed off on the older people. Occasionally there were other guests, like Hans Arp and other artists. Once, when the students were giving their talks, Giedion asked him, "What do you think, Arp?" Arp took a box of matches out of his pocket—he was a smoker—threw the matches on the table and said, "Now that's beautiful!" Then he picked them all up, tossed them once more, and said, "Now it's beautiful again." This impressed me deeply, and, much later, the insight into the laws of chance affected my work as well.

DS      And what about Carola Giedion-Welcker?

RH      She told us a lot about new books and she knew many important artists.
        After I finished my education, I was Willy Rotzler's assistant for a short time when he was the director of the Museum of Arts and Crafts in Zurich. I helped him mount exhibitions, for example one in 1952 about applied art from Denmark, through which I met Danish designers.

DS      And how did you get interested in art?

RH     The director of the School of Arts and Crafts was Johannes Itten, who came from the Bauhaus but who propagated esoteric theories in his lectures. He already did that at the Bauhaus—breathing exercises complemented his theory of color.

DS     You studied at the School of Arts and Crafts and not at the ETH Department of Architecture, is that right?

RH     Yes, but I was in touch with some professors at the ETH. One person sticks out in particular: Sigfried Giedion. He had gathered a coterie of students around him and conducted a salon in his villa in the Doldertal overlooking Zurich. We would go there for tea and everyone had to give a short talk. We would discuss current issues, like the theory of proportion or new music and we learned about a lot of different things. For instance, Wladimir Vogel, whose speech choirs were critically acclaimed at the time, introduced us to twelve-tone composition and Hans Kayser lectured on his esoteric theory of an all-encompassing harmony derived from the planetary system. He instructed us and we all built a monochord, a kind of one-stringed instrument.

TH     Kayser's ideas were also important for architects in those days; my aunt gave me a book by him when I started studying.

dam, the Kunstnijverheidsschool Quellinus, and through him I met Willem Sandberg, who was the director of the Stedelijk Museum and who mounted the first De Stijl retrospective in 1951. I had the opportunity to work as an intern and go through letters, sketches, and other documents, basketfuls that had been collected at various estates and brought to the museum.

DS      After the war, Sandberg turned the Stedelijk into Europe's leading museum…

RH      … and the Concertgebouw Orchestra was also in Amsterdam, not just the canals. A drawing by Theo van Doesburg had been delivered to the museum from somebody's estate for the De Stijl exhibition. It was badly damaged and had brown spots. I bought Talens paints, mixed them and tried to retouch every single spot. Years later, at an exhibition at MoMA, we saw the drawing again and it looked terrible. It was the one I had "restored"; the paper and my work on it had become discolored and it looked even worse than before.

DS      Acquaintance with Klee and the De Stijl artists meant that you already knew about important representatives of modernism. Did you have teachers in Zurich who drew your attention to such artists?

TH     It was primarily about friendship; we knew the artists and then things took off from there. And it was also a kind of balance for our own work as architects. We always had clients and the artists were at the other end of the spectrum; they were free to do what they wanted, without obligations. Since we did our creative work on commission, that was an exciting aspect for us.

DS     Did you discover a liking for the fine arts through your education or had you earlier already become interested?

RH     For me it started in my early teens. At a Klee exhibition in Kunsthaus Zürich in 1948. I was completely overwhelmed. Admission was free on Sunday afternoons and since I lived nearby, I would spend whole afternoons wandering around looking at the permanent collection. It was like the way other people go to the movies—uncharted territory and different from home.

DS     Were you introduced to works of art at home?

RH     Not at home, but before I graduated I went to Amsterdam on a student exchange and I also spent a few months in Sweden. Gerrit Rietveld was director of the School of Arts and Crafts in Amster-

DS      Walking into your apartment, there are mirrors everywhere, and it's slightly disorientating. I remember how you once said that mirrors can be used to destroy, stretch, and change reality. In a different sense, I think the same thing applies to the drawings and pictures that cover the walls, and to the sculptures standing wherever there's any space left between the books and furnishings. Is there a principle behind the hang? Is it often changed?

TH      We've always tried to hang the pictures so that they have an inner coherence, but also so that their formats correlate—one work should talk to the other. Hanging them has always been hard work because when we renovate a room in the apartment or when several works are away on loan, we have to rehang them.

DS      Do you think of yourselves as art collectors?

TH      Not really.

RH      When you get old and find yourself surrounded by the things that you are interested in and connect with, then the result is something like a collection.

# A LIFE WITH ART AND ARTISTS
## TRIX [TH] AND ROBERT HAUSSMANN [RH]
## IN CONVERSATION
## WITH DIETER SCHWARZ [DS]

# EDITION

# PATRICK

# FREY

# N° 3 3 8

ARTISTS

TRIX + ROBERT
HAUSSMANN
IN CONVERSATION WITH
DIETER SCHWARZ

IM GESPRÄCH MIT
HAUSSMANN
TRIX + ROBERT
KÜNSTLER:INNEN
KUNST +
EINLEBEN MIT